GUGGENHEIM BILBAO MUSEOA

Joseba Zulaika Ph.D. received his Licentiate in Philosophy from the University of Deusto-Bilbao, Spain, in 1975; his M.A. in Social Anthropology from Memorial University of Newfoundland, Canada, in 1977; and his Ph.D. in Cultural Anthropology from Princeton University in 1982. He is currently the director of the Center for Basque Studies at the University of Nevada, Reno.

He has published the following books relevant to this course: *Tratado Estético-Ritual Vasco* (Baroja, San Sebastián, 1987); *Basque Violence: Metaphor and Sacrament* (University of Nevada, Reno, 1988); *Del Cromañón al Carnaval: los vascos como museo antropológico* (Erein, San Sebastián, 1996); (With William Douglass) *Terror and Taboo: The Follies, Fables, and Faces of Terrorism* (Routledge, New York, 1996); *Crónica de una seducción: el Museo Guggenheim-Bilbao* (Nerea, Madrid, 1997). He has also published various articles on the Guggenheim Museum in professional journals.

His primary research interests include: Bilbao's Guggenheim Museum and urban renewal; Basque culture and politics; the international discourse of terrorism; diasporic and global cultures; and theories of symbolism, ritual, and discourse.

Joseba Zulaika

Guggenheim Bilbao Museoa
Museums, Architecture, and City Renewal

Basque Textbooks Series

Center for Basque Studies
University of Nevada, Reno

This book was published with generous financial support from the Basque Government.

Library of Congress Cataloging-in-Publication Data

Zulaika, Joseba.

Guggenheim Bilbao Museoa : museums, architecture, and city renewal / Joseba Zulaika.

p. cm.

Includes bibliographical references and index.

ISBN 1-877802-06-9 (paperback)

ISBN 1-877802-07-7 (hardcover)

ISBN 1-877802-08-5 (compact disk)

1. Museo Guggenheim Bilbao. 2. Urban renewal—Spain—Bilbao. 3. Tourism and art—Spain–Bilbao. 4. Bilbao (Spain)—Buildings, structures, etc. I. Title: Museums, architecture, and city renewal. II. Title.

HC387.P28 G65 2002

330.946'608—dc21

2002014096

Published by the Center for Basque Studies
University of Nevada, Reno /322
Reno, Nevada 89557-0012.

Printed in the United States of America.

CONTENTS

1 · Postindustrial Bilbao

Old city in a global world

BILBAO WAS a "medieval villa" (founded in the year 1300 by Don Diego López de Haro). Then it became a "commercial villa" (after the establishment of its consulate in 1511). Then, in the second half of the last century, it grew into the proud regional "industrial city" we all know. But a new millennium has dawned, and now, since the middle 1990s, a new "postindustrial Bilbao" is being reborn from the ashes of its industrial ruins.

A massive transformation of infrastructure and process of urban regeneration is under way that is turning Bilbao into a service-oriented, culturally attractive city. The signature project of the transformation, Frank Gehry's spectacular Guggenheim Bilbao Museoa, is an international star, but is just one part of the postindustrial reinvention of the city. As it undergoes the painful yet exhilarating metamorphosis from industrial ruin to architectural gem, Bilbao is opening itself up to tourism and globalized culture, but by doing so presents unique challenges to students of Basque society and culture.

The great turn-of-the-century Spanish philosopher and writer Miguel de Unamuno wrote of the Nervión River, which anchors his native Bilbao,

You are, Nervión, the history of the Villa,
you her past and her future, you are
memory always turning into hope
and on your firm riverbed
a fleeing flow.

The foundational charter granted the medieval villa exclusive jurisdictional rights to Nervión trade. The river has supplied Bilbao's history, wealth, and central

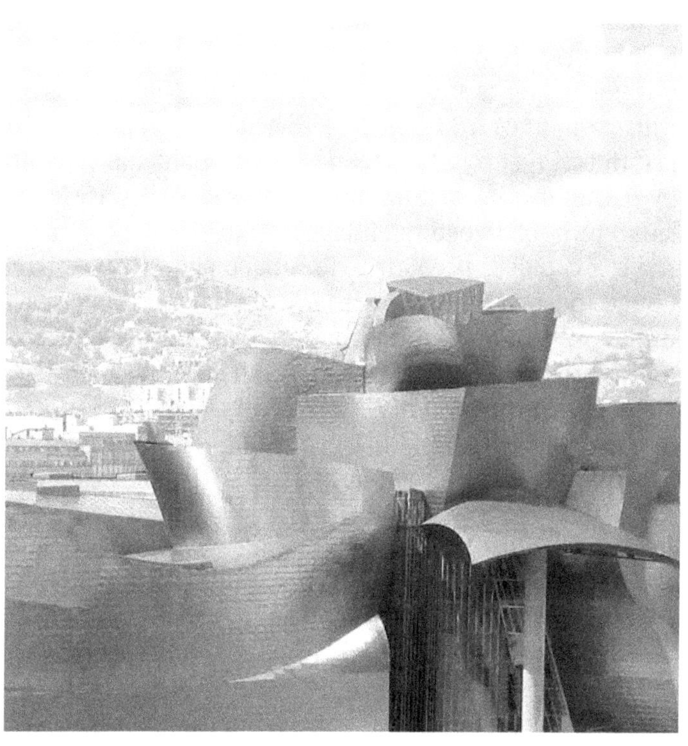

Frank Gehry's Guggenheim Bilbao Museoa proclaims the postindustrial reinvention of a city.
Photo: Ibon Aranberri.

metaphor. Bilbao provided the natural port for exports and a wide window on the world.

Bilbao was doubly blessed with a seaport and vast mineral wealth. The import of this blessing has been particularly clear in the last 150 years of industrial boom, during which the River's left bank became the home of Spain's largest iron and steel industries.

A wasteland of industrial ruins is almost all that remains of that dynamic industrial period. The ongoing massive redevelopment offers testimony that the generous, dark river is still very much the city's engine. As Bilbao emerges from the debris accumulated during the last tide of history, the city of 360,000 people has, mostly by natural forces, begun to rediscover something of the small town of 18,000 it left behind 150 years ago. During the last two decades of decline, 75,000 people have abandoned the city. But Bilbao is far from having abandoning her central role in international business. Her capacity for high-stakes risk taking remains undiminished. And she remains the city about which Bertolt Brecht wrote, "How beautiful, how beautiful, how beautiful is the moon of Bilbao, the most beautiful city of the continent." Her "tough city" aesthetic has seduced many internationally known artists, notably Richard Serra and Frank Gehry. This seduction is now perhaps Bilbao's greatest asset; in this arena Bilbao, by architectural spectacle and the sheer will to challenge all odds, is transforming herself in ways unimaginable a short time ago.

IN *ABANDOIBARRA*, right across from the University of Deusto, a grand titanium-skinned white whale has run aground. Or is it a pirate's old galleon suddenly resurfaced? Gehry's masterpiece is the now undisputed emblem of a reinvigorated city unwilling to fade away with the demise of its blast furnaces, the *Altos Hornos de Vizcaya*, famed industrial engine and once-fiery symbol of the region's booming economy. The volcano of the left bank is now mostly extinguished, but the sunset's yellow colors are captured and reflected on the titanium scales of Gehry's pallid cetacean. The *New York Times* proclaimed it "A miracle!" The real miracle, of course, is the resolve of the Bilbainos not to let their city's proverbial fire and flourish be extinguished.

Ashen debris, white smoke, black water, red slag—a generous supply of dirt of all colors and elements had become Bilbao's constant companion and emblem. Her distinctive aesthetic accomplishment has been to turn her ugliness into a badge of honor, an object of beauty, for those willing to contemplate with eyes uncontaminated by pastoral nostalgia. Now that the smoking chimneys are gone, even dirt is in shorter supply, and the tourists have begun to arrive. The decades of heavy industrial exploitation had turned the Nervión into a black meandering sewer upon which the Bilbainos had learned to turn their backs. They no longer need to avert their eyes from the prodigious river, the soul of their history and identity. On the contrary, Bilbao is transforming her riverfront once again into the center of the city. An ambitious $1.5 billion urban renewal plan is being implemented, focusing upon the expansion of the port and airport, creation of a subway, and planning for a transport hub. A new development on the riverfront, called Abandoibarra, will include a convention center and concert hall, *Euskalduna*, as well as the spectacular Guggenheim.

TWO OF THESE major projects are emblematic of the new Bilbao: Foster's sleek costly subway, which, besides its practical advantages, symbolizes the city's new modernity; and Gehry's voluptuous and optimistic Guggenheim Museum. The museum has overshadowed all other renewal projects and drawn the international attention Bilbao craves.

This is as great a historical transformation as one could expect from Bilbao's *fin de millennium*. It signals the city's willingness to unburden herself of all the sins of the industrial revolution and the ensuing environmental degradation. With the hegemony of mining and iron industries overthrown, the sky free of the dark drifting clouds pumped into it by the smoking chimneys, it is no longer taboo to look at the river.

The Nervión River was first bridged long before the villa was founded in 1300. The construction of the San Antón Bridge was a Promethean attempt to arch worlds apart: land and shore, river and sea, interior and exterior, past and future, left and right. It is this tradition of bridging the seemingly impossible—suspension bridges floating in air and drawbridges opening up their mandibles to the sky in a big yawn as the cargo files surreptitiously by, these tenuous and temporary structural rites of passage, yet complicated and enduring works of arrogant engineering—that sustained Bilbao's self-invented image of a synthesis of warring elements, a historical linkage between the seemingly irreconcilable worlds of the villa and its hinterland, the rural and urban economies, aristocratic and proletarian lives, and Basque and European interests.

AFTER THE easternmost bridge in the Deusto neighborhood, fifteen kilometers on the right and left riverbanks from the city to the sea were uncompromised by any link, with the single exception of the suspension bridge in Portugalete. But times are changing and the river has been crisscrossed by several new bridges (*Rontegi, Euskalduna, Zubizuri*), and others are in the planning stages. The one bridge that really matters must connect Bilbao with entities both more virtual (so-called global culture) and more concrete (Wall Street) than anything spanned so far. The Basque president's visit to Wall Street to deliver a $20 million check for the Guggenheim Museum franchise is a statement that leaves few doubts in this regard.

Bridging the interior's provincial *tierra llana* ("flat

land") with the port-centered, open-to-the world villa was no small feat. Now, however, the only measure of success is the bridging of transatlantic distances—New York at one end and Bilbao at the other—facilitating traffic in modern art and museum franchises. The Romanesque arches of the San Antón Bridge, medieval symbol of a proud Bilbao, are now complemented by the postindustrial city establishing herself as the key port and fundamental artistic *point de repére* (reference point) of the so-called "Atlantic Arch" stretching between Santiago de Compostela and Bourdeaux. Welcome to the newly imagined global postmodern space of late capitalism.

BUT THERE is much bridging to be done at home as well between the two riverbanks, the two languages, and the two millennia. Issues of violence, nationality, class, gender, and language continue to polarize Bilbao society. She appears uneasily perched between a mythology of the past, which successfully deployed an ethnographic identity of premodern Basque enigmatic uniqueness, and a mythology of the future, which looks to global markets and the delirious glamour of New York for the inspiration of a new postethnic identity.

The discourse of urban regeneration works particularly well in fostering a sense of new direction. It embraces economic as well as environmental, cultural, social, and symbolic components. Leisure activities and so-called "cultural industries attain great significance in regenerating urban centers. The distinctions among "art," "communication," "culture," and "entertainment" disappear. Urban regeneration led by leisure and cultural industries has been attempted with uneven results in various European and American cities. Not only yuppie tourists, the discourse reassures us, but also Bilbao's unemployed, youth, migrants, and other marginalized people will benefit from such cultural industries. The argument is that star-quality architecture is the condition for the economic renewal that will bring jobs and prestige back to the city.

In the beginning was architecture—*arché*, or foundation. In classical aesthetic theory, architecture is the first art. Salvation by architecture is the cornerstone of the new regenerationist ideology in Bilbao. Due to its dependence on public funds, architecture tends more than the other arts to be manipulated for ideological purposes. Bilbao provides what may well prove to be the grandest example of architecture as ideology and spectacle. The ideological use of architecture is based on the uncontested assumption that public power must invest massively in *emblematic* buildings conceived by star architects. Emblematic, that is, of ideas of progress, culture, class, equality, and peace.

THIS IS THE time to visit and study Bilbao. Gehry's masterpiece is an architectural triumph amidst the postindustrial ruins of the Nervión. This is architecture that provides cause for celebration. It has been likened to a whale, a ship, an artichoke, a mermaid, a waterfall, a flower, a fish, Marilyn Monroe, and a chopped-up Chinese paper dragon. It has been hailed as the signature building of the late twentieth century.

This is also the time to realize the potential rewards of turning Bilbao into a privileged topic of research and writing. Ruination and rebirth, the end of times and the beginning of times, are historical processes meriting the scrutiny of urban and cultural studies. Some of the discourses deserving particular attention are:

1. The ruined postindustrial city turned into the postmodern model of an architecturally imprinted city
2. Urban planning and regeneration
3. Architecture

---

4. Museum culture
5. Globalization
6. Postindustrialism
7. Migration
8. International art markets
9. Cultural industries
10. Anthropology
11. History

Lesson one

REQUIRED READING

Eduardo J. Glass, "Historical Background" (Chapter 1, *Bilbao's Modern Business Elite*, Univ. of Nevada Press, Reno, 1997).

SUGGESTED READING

Frederick Buell, "The Three Worlds" (Chapter 1, *National Culture and the New Global System*, Johns Hopkins Press, Baltimore, 1994).

LEARNING GOALS

1. Situate Bilbao geographically and historically.
2. Introduce the global view of economic and cultural history.
3. Raise initial questions regarding the dilemmas, complexities, challenges, and opportunities presented to traditional cultures and postindustrial economies by a globalized world.
4. Recognize the necessities of urban and economic renewal within this newly globalized world.

WRITTEN LESSON FOR SUBMISSION

Please write a two- to three-page essay on one of the topics below.

1. Describe some of the basic dilemmas faced by traditional cultures when confronted with the new wave of globalization.
2. What is your view of the tensions between "universal civilization" and "national cultures"?
3. Is Bilbao's premodern history a closed economic unit or cultural independent configuration in any sense? Or is it, rather, a global construction?
4. To the degree that Bilbao has been at the forefront of Basque commerce, industry, and urban life, what are the implications of such global reach for Basque culture in general?

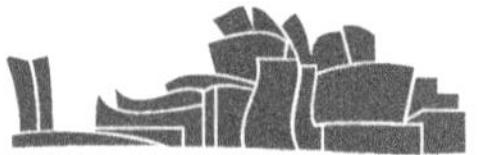

2 · Bilbao and the world economic system

The English connection

BILBAO IS located in the Spanish province of Vizcaya. It is the birthplace of both Basque nationalism and Spanish socialism. Its history, social makeup, and political significance underscore the role of serving for centuries as the commercial center for its rural Basque hinterland as well as, for the last 150 years, a mining and industrial magnet for Spanish migrants. To better appreciate the historical differences attached to urban city formations, one must be able to situate Bilbao within its larger geographical setting.

"Country" (in the sense of land and nation) and "city" are very powerful words, argues Raymond Williams. The "country way of life" encompassed hunters, herders, farmers, and factory farmers, as well as their various social organizations. Likewise, cities have a wide variety of aspects from which they can be assessed: administrative base, state capital, religious center, market-town, port and mercantile depot, and site of industrial concentration. For centuries Bilbao was a small mercantile port, but since the turn of the last century it has been an industrial city. Because of this wide variety of qualities, cities are characterized by their heightened sense of possibility.

In an otherwise "pastoral" Basque society, Bilbao has represented the counter-pastoral. The pastoral implies a particular structure of customs, beliefs, and sentiments tied to the epic of animal husbandry. Agriculture and trading are part of a way of life in which effort and prudence are primary virtues. The myth of a golden age is always close. The pastoral has a long literary tradition going back to the Hellenistic world. The Virgilian arcadia, the idyllic world, the utopian vision of a Second

Coming, and the restoration of the golden age are all part of this pastoral worldview.

Basques, widely depicted as shepherds, have had their share of pastoral experiences, but the main industrial and urban Basque center shatters the basis for such a collective representation. All traditions are selective, the pastoral as much as any other. In such traditions the transition from the rural to the industrial is portrayed as a kind of fall. The power of this myth has been extraordinary not only in Basque nationalist politics but in modern social thought as well.

Bilbao's mining tradition represents the counter-pastoral. It goes back at least to Roman times, when Pliny wrote about a "mountain of iron" near Bilbao. The ferrerías (small furnaces fueled by charcoal and powered by water) kept the mining tradition alive throughout the Middle Ages, but it wasn't until the second half of nineteenth century, when approximately 100 million tons of ore were extracted from Mount Triano, that Pliny was finally proved undeniably right. Bilbao became one of Europe's busiest seaports and attracted immigrants from across Spain. Bilbao had suddenly appeared at the industrial center of the European capitalist system.

WOLF PROVIDES the world historical perspective from which to understand Bilbao's role. From the fifteenth century on, European soldiers and sailors, merchants in the service of "God and profit," provided wide-ranging military and naval support while furnishing commodities to overseas suppliers in exchange for goods to be sold as commodities at home. The outcome was the creation of a commercial network on a global scale. As a result, for three and a half centuries Spain and Portugal divided South America, Central America, Mexico and parts of North America among themselves,

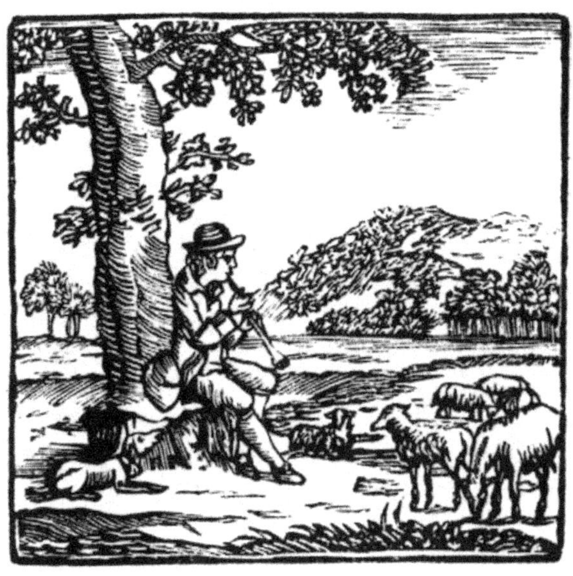

Beware the myth of a golden age. In an otherwise "pastoral" Basque society, Bilbao has represented the counter-pastoral.
Engraving: school of Thomas Bewick (1753–1828.)

---

while England and France claimed the Antilles and most of North America.

The growth of European commerce encountered its own limits and contradictions. The state had to be transformed from a tributary structure to a structure of support for capitalist enterprise. The breakthrough from mercantile domination to the capitalist mode of production took place in England. Why England? There is no one answer. Wolf points to the transformation of agriculture into business, the high degree of interaction among commercial agents, the weakening of the aristocracy, and the fact that peasant lands were converted into leaseholds.

MECHANIZATION WAS central to the industrial revolution. Inventors sought to make spinning more productive, and by 1830 Watt's steam engine was transforming a manual operation into a mechanical one where one mule spinner could work as many as 1,600 spindles. The new labor conditions forced females and juveniles into the workforce, and by 1838 only 23 percent of textile factory workers were adult men. The English textile industry gave birth to a new mode of production. Capitalists could buy machines and hire workers to operate them in exchange for wages. Thus, capital could control the means of production and rearrange them in the service of profitability. At the same time, capital began a process of international migration.

In addition to machines and labor, an important aspect of this international expansion had to do with raw materials. Factories needed materials from faraway regions of the world. One of these raw materials, iron ore, was crucial for developing the new railroad and shipbuilding industries. Its iron ore made Bilbao a strategic partner with the British Empire); with capitalist specialization, economic dependence became worldwide. The movement of commodities began to reach out over the globe, necessitating the founding of an articulated system of capitalist and non-capitalist relations of production linked by relations of exchange that were dominated by capitalist accumulation. One of the consequences of the new worldwide system was the enslavement of about 12 million Africans for labor in the New

World (an additional 36 million died at sea). The native American people, hard to enslave in their own land and a threat because of their belief in land stewardship rather than ownership, were allowed and encouraged to dwindle from an estimated original population between 12 and 18 million to 500,000 by 1900.

As described by Glass, in Vizcaya (Bilbao's province) a small group of owners took advantage of their early acquaintance with the iron trade to control the most productive mines. Production increased substantially. Bilbao's iron, with its rich metallic content, was ideal for the Bessemer converter (in use in Bilbao since it was invented in 1856), and could be extracted cheaply. As well, Vizcaya was relatively close to England. A strong relationship grew between Bilbao and Great Britain. More than two-thirds of British imports of ore came from Bilbao.

HENRY BESSEMER'S converter allowed cheap production of steel in vast quantities. Bilbao's output of iron ore went from 55,000 tons in 1861 to 2,684,000 tons in 1880, and to 6,496,000 in 1898. The fact that Great Britain, the world's imperial power, imported two-thirds of her iron ore from Bilbao (representing 65–75 percent of Bilbao's annual exports) gives a good sense of Vizcaya's crucial role in the global capitalist system of late nineteenth century. Foreign companies came to Bilbao not only as buyers of ore, but also as backers and direct participants in the exploitation of the mines. Investments in the iron and steel industries, railroads, and the harbor, proved that international capital was crucial to the region's industrialization. In fact, the two most important foreign companies, the Orconera Iron Ore Co. and the Société Franco-Belge des Mines de Somorrostro, were multinationals. Orconera Iron Ore Co. was formed in 1873 by the association of the Ybarras, two British pioneers of the Bessemer converter, and the German industrial firm Krupp. (The Ybarras were also founding partners in the Société Franco-Belge, formed in 1876.) Why did the Ybarras associate with foreign partners? Essentially, to spread the risks in uncertain times.

The harbor was a key part of the infrastructure and was renovated and financed by private (national and foreign) and public funds. Railroads connecting three mines with the harbor were built in the 1870s.

Although massive infusions of foreign capital were necessary to fund the modern exploitation of the mines, it would be wrong to conclude that the mineral resources were simply colonized by foreigners. The Ybarra's income, for example, was derived from royalties and dividends and represented more than 50 percent of the Orconera's profits, a much higher amount than they derived from the 25 percent of the company's stock that they owned. Glass estimates that overall the local business elite pocketed between 56.3 percent and 74 percent of all the mining profits. Although foreign companies extracted 40 percent of Vizcaya's iron from 1880 to 1900, the advanced exploitation of the mines proved a good symbiotic relationship, which provided, besides profits, a healthy transfer of British technology. Without foreign capital Vizcaya's industrialization would have been much more problematic.

Lesson two

REQUIRED READING

Eduardo Glass, "The Development of the Mining Industry" (Chapter 2, Bilbao's Modern Business Elite, Univ. of Nevada, Reno, 1997).

Eric Wolf, "Industrial Revolution" (Chapter 9, Europe and the People Without History, Univ. of California Press, Berkeley, 1982)

SUGGESTED READING

Raymond Williams, "Country and City" and "Pastoral and Counter-Pastoral" (Chapters 1 and 3, The Country and the City, Oxford Univ. Press, New York, 1973).

LEARNING GOALS

1. Understand Bilbao's history within the contexts of European and world history.
2. Recognize the dialectics of the economic-cultural relationship between Bilbao and its Basque hinterland.
3. Appreciate the connections between the English industrial revolution and Bilbao.
4. Assess the symbiotic relationship between local and global capital.

WRITTEN LESSON FOR SUBMISSION

Please write a two- to three-page essay on one of the topics below.

1. Situate Bilbao's industrial development in the overall European economic context.
2. Assess the widespread pastoral representations of the Basques.
3. Was Bilbao at the core or at the periphery of the world capitalist system?
4. Do you find colonial interpretations of Basque history valid or not?

3 · Industrialization

THE PANORAMA of the mountains ... rising above the sea and the Nervión valley, smoking with a hundred chimneys, forms a spectacle that is so stunning as to become unforgettable," wrote Max Weber to his mother from Bilbao at the turn of the twentieth century.

During the first half of the nineteenth century, Vizcaya lagged behind other Spanish provinces in modern industrial development. Though it was primarily a rural province, agriculture alone was not sufficient to feed all the Vizcayans, and food had to be imported. Explosive growth took place after 1876, after many other modernization attempts from 1840 to 1875.

In 1856 Bilbao ranked tenth in shipping tonnage among commercial Spanish ports; by the mid-1860s it was second only to Barcelona. Bilbao's ascent was difficult. Setbacks included the decline of iron and wool (traditional materials for export) during the first part of the century and the First Carlist War of succession to the Spanish throne in the early 1830s. Andalucía established more advanced factories. Bilbao lost the right to import duty-free products and became fully integrated into the Spanish market. The integration, however, opened new trade opportunities with the Spanish colonies, Cuba, Puerto Rico, and the Philippines. Imports grew during the 1840s, 1850s, and 1860s with Great Britain (textiles, machinery, drugs, and chemical products), France (silk and textiles), and Norway (codfish) providing approximately 75 percent of the imports. Bilbao exported grain, flour, wine, and iron ore, with grain and flour amounting to 72 percent of the exports from 1858 to 1866. Bilbao's shipyards enjoyed great prosperity during the 1850s and 1860s. Total tonnage went from 30,000 in

1847 to 68,200 in 1858 (739 vessels). Still, Bilbao's port was a distant second to the neighboring port of Santander.

Banking and insurance was another growth industry of the 1850s. The Union Bilbaina insurance company was founded in 1850 by forty of the wealthiest Bilbao merchants. By 1861 seven insurance companies operated in Bilbao. Banco Bilbao was established in 1857 and had the privilege of issuing paper money that served as legal tender. Large partnerships provided the advantage of reducing risk without which the ambitious project of constructing the railroad line between Bilbao and Tudela (necessary to maintain the Castilian market, and finally completed in 1863) would never have been undertaken. Financed mostly by foreign countries, the Spanish railroad network was extended from 500 to 5,000 kilometers between 1855 and 1865, with most of the materials imported from Great Britain. The Bilbao-Tudela railroad was financed with local capital.

MODERNIZATION SPREAD to the manufacturing industries of the mid-1800s. Merchants dominated the iron industry until the 1830s, and by the late 1840s there were 621 mills in Vizcaya. The *ferrerías*, virtually unchanged since the Middle Ages, were finally obsolete. In 1848 the iron factory Santa Ana built the first Vizcayan blast furnace. The modern giants facilitated the separation of the smelting and refining processes and producing as much as one hundred times the output of *ferrerías*. The blast furnace of Nuestra Señora del Carmen followed in 1855. Lack of coal was a serious hindrance to these iron factories. The neighboring region of Asturias produced more iron wrought than Vizcaya in the mid-1860s. The cost of iron ore was 8.75 pesetas in Vizcaya versus 14.87 in Asturias; yet the cost of coke was 19.75 pesetas in Asturias versus 54.25 in Vizcaya. The failure to find coal near Bilbao forced the Ybarras and Co. to export the mineral from Asturias or Great Britain.

Bilbao's prosperity fostered urban renewal projects. Water conduits had to be built by the 1860s for the needs of Bilbao's inhabitants.

AS THE LOCAL iron industry was breaking away from the obsolete *ferrerías,* the city began to become one of the most important ports of Spain. The population grew at double the nationwide rate from 1859 to 1900. In 1887, 41.5 percent of the population of Valmaseda, 73 percent of Baracaldo, and 38.2 percent of Bilbao were immigrants and the industrial and service sectors equaled those in the primary sector, agriculture. As late as 1900, two-thirds of the active population in Spain were in the agriculture; this proportion was almost reversed in Vizcaya.

In 1901, the worth of new companies in Vizcaya was 483 million pesetas. This represented 55 percent of all investments in Spain. Where did these investments come from? Some historians emphasize the importance of the capital accumulated through mining and its investment in other industries; others underplay the direct contribution of mining. Montero, for instance, calculates that between 1878 and 1898 the mining profits were on the order of 405 million pesetas. Glass puts the number at 324 million, and not all of these profits went to Vizcayan businessmen. Not all of the 240 million pesetas in profits of the local entrepreneurs were accounted for by the Vizcayan investments during 1880–1900. According to the British consul, for example, from 1886–1899, around 420 million pesetas were invested in new companies. These do not include three of the most important steel factories, the renewal of the local fleet, and other companies founded during the 1880s, all of which would require at least another 100

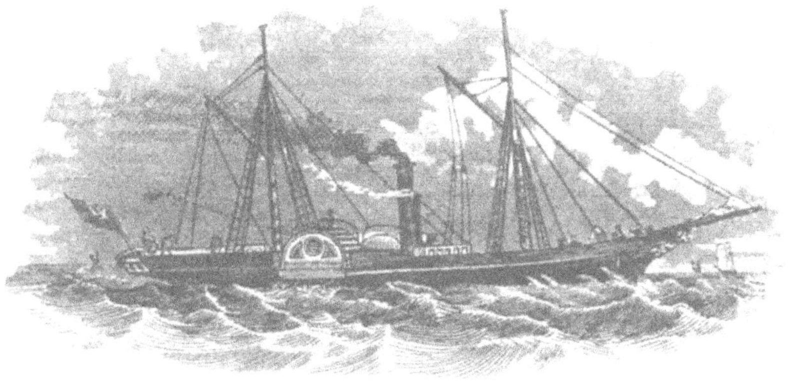

The Basque shipping indusry attracted vast capital. Bilbaos fleet doubled between 1895 and 1900.
Engraving: ES & Robinson's

---

million pesetas. Glass concludes that mining profits can account at best for 60 percent of the investments. The rest of the money could only come from local savings or from outside businesses. Fernández de Pinedo and others have called attention to these outside investors, in particular the 57 percent of *Altos Hornos de Bilbao* steel factory's capital that came from outside the province. The largest stockholder of *La Vizcaya* was a shipping company of Basque businessmen based in Liverpool.

The modernization of the iron and steel industry took place between 1879 and 1882 with the establishment of three modern factories with powerful blast furnaces fueled by coke: *San Francisco, Altos Hornos de Bilbao,* and *La Vizcaya*. By 1881, *San Francisco*'s four blast furnaces were producing about 36,000 tons of iron, almost a third of the total Spanish production. The other two factories soon followed the success of *San Francisco*. *Altos Hornos* was the continuation of two Ybarra and Co. factories; they secured the exclusive rights to the Bessemer converter in Spain. *La Vizcaya*, promoted by Victor Chavarri, was the creation of several prominent mine-owning families. The three factories enjoyed special arrangements that reduced the costs of transportation of the ore. Their location on the Nervión River facilitated the import of British coal, the return freight for the ore exported to England, and the cost of coal dropped dramatically in Bilbao. Vizcaya began to dominate the manufacture of iron and steel in Spain. Its share of Spain's total production increased to 66 percent between 1880 and 1913 (from 23 percent between 1861 and 1879). Vizcayan businessmen also promoted the extraction of other minerals such as lead, coal, sulfur, and copper throughout Spain.

BILBAO COULD produce steel at one of the lowest prices in Europe. How much was exported? According to Pinedo 30 percent; according to Portilla 60 percent. Italy absorbed 65 percent of the bars between 1887 and 1890; Germany, 9 percent; France, 7.25 percent.

Although the furnaces were the main evidence of modernization, railroad lines, chemical factories, and shipping companies were also rapidly appearing. Between 1880 and 1885, new railway lines parallel to both banks of the Nervión connected Bilbao to the seacoast. Bilbao's Sociedad Española de Dinnertime owned the rights to the Nobel patent to produce dynamite in Spain. In 1878, an oil refinery was established on the banks of the Nervión.

Between 1880 and 1885 the shipping industry attracted 30.3 million pesetas, a vast amount of capital, larger than the combined capital of *La Vizcaya* and *Altos Hornos*. This large investment was related to the massive exports of minerals from Bilbao. During the mid-1890s the Spanish government requested that three vessels be built at the shipyard Astillerons de Nervión. They were built successfully, but sank in Cuba during the Spanish-American War. Such promotion of national industries was extended to other companies as well. Shipping continued to attract capital, and grew from 90,000 tons in 1885 to 156,000 tons ten years later. Bilbao's biggest shipping company, Sota and Aznar, was formed in this period. Assisted by the demands of the Boer War, Bilbao's fleet increased another 50 percent between 1895 and 1900, becoming in the process the largest in the country and accounting for about one-half of the total Spanish tonnage.

THE BILBAO STOCK Exchange was established in 1890 and increased in value 50 percent in its first five years. Banking was restructured at the turn of the century, and attracted almost 100 million pesetas. In 1901 Banco de Bilbao and Banco de Comercio merged, while new banks were forming. The seven local banks had a combined capital of 98 million pesetas. Only three of them survived the 1901 crash. Two of them, Banco de Bilbao and Banco de Vizcaya, were among the five largest Spanish banks until they merged in 1988.

The metallurgic industry attracted less capital than banking, shipping, and mining, but continued to grow and remained the backbone of the Vizcayan manufacturing sector. In 1901 *Altos Hornos de Bilbao*, *La Vizcaya*, and *La Iberia* merged to create a new company, *Altos*

Hornos de Vizcaya, with a combined capital of 32.7 million pesetas. The tendency towards industrial concentration continued during the first decades of the century. Many of these firms were de facto monopolies, protected from foreign competition with high tariffs, at the expense of Spanish consumers.

In 1929, although Basques constituted a mere 3 percent of Spain's population, Basque capital represented 25 percent of Spanish banking resources, 38 percent of the investment in shipyards, 40 percent of the stock in engineering and electrical construction firms, 68 percent of the funds dedicated to shipping companies, and 62 percent of the investments in steel factories.

Lesson three

REQUIRED READING

Eduardo Glass, "General Economic Development" (Chapter 3, Bilbao's Modern Business Elite, Univ. of Nevada, Reno, 1997).

Max Weber, letter to his mother from Bilbao

SUGGESTED READING

Erik Wolf, "The New Laborers" (Chapter 12, *Europe and the People Without History*, Univ. of California Press, Berkeley, 1982).

LEARNING GOALS

1. Become acquainted with the basic facts of Bilbao's industrialization.
2. Identify the spread of capital from mining to metallurgy, shipping, banking, and other industries.
3. Assess Bilbao's industrial development and its relationship to the European global capitalist system.

WRITTEN LESSON FOR SUBMISSION

Please write a two- to three-page essay on one of the topics below.

1. Could Bilbao's successful industrialization have taken place with local capital alone?
2. What technological changes made it possible to transform the medieval industry of iron works and foundries into modern factories with blast furnaces?
3. What changes were brought about by the industrialization process in the distribution of the working population and the various economic sectors?
4. What is the most remarkable feature of Bilbao's general economic development?

4 · The *ensanche* urban reinvention

A new city for a new elite

THE GLOBAL PROCESS of industrialization deeply transformed Spain and forced new urban planning aimed at controlling the new demographic growth. In several Spanish cities, including Madrid (1860), San Sebasti'an (1864), and Bilbao (1876), new ensanches (enlargements) were approved. New means of transportation had to be built, drastically changing the urban structure of the cities. It didn't prove viable to simply reform the old city quarters. Ideas of defending the city by means of walls and fortifications had become obsolete. The transportation options engendered by the steam engine marked a historical breakthrough.

By midcentury, forces that would lead to the growth and transformation of traditional Bilbao were at work. Mining and transportation had increased dramatically and during the 1860s several railways were being built. Bilbao's population almost tripled in just thirty years (from 17,923 in 1857 to 50,772 in 1887). This growth was due, in part, to the annexation of the neighboring villas of Begoña and Abando in 1870.

The need for an "enlargement" was self-evident. The first *Ensanche* project was carried out in 1861 (see map on next page). In 1872 the city commissioned engineers Alzola and Hoffmeyer and architect Achucarro to do another *Ensanche*. Pablo Alzola had been mayor of the city, as well as president of the Provincial Council and general director of the Public Works. Both a politician and technician, he personified the changing Bilbao ethos and the kind of modernizing promoter called into existence at the end of the nineteenth century by the industrialization needs of the new bourgeoisie.

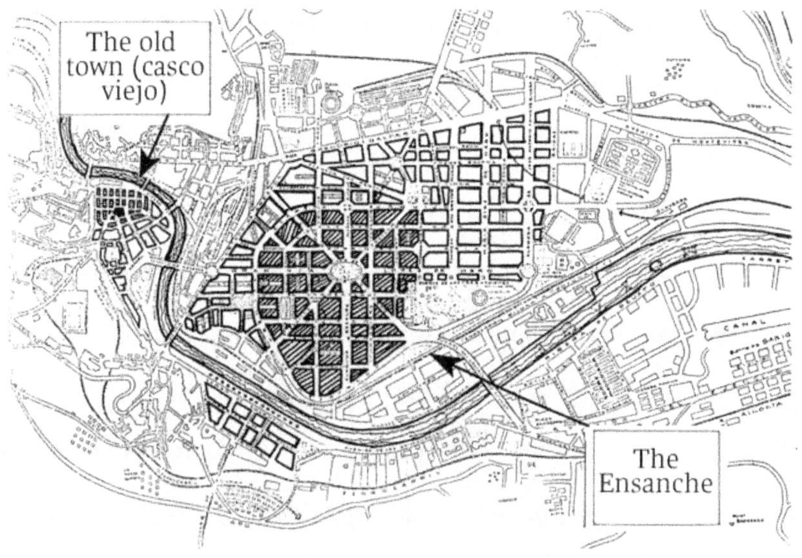

Rapid industrialization changed Bilbao. By the 1860s a new city was planned, the ensanche "enlargement." Houses had been built and streets laid without a strict, cental design. The new area of planned prosperity was more orderly.
Map by permission of Bilbao central archives.

As pointed out by Arpal and Minondo ("El Bilbao de la industrialization: Una ciudad para una élite," *Saioak* 2(2): 31–68), such *Ensanches* went beyond a mere enlargement of the urban soil. They entailed a new conception of global social relations by taking into account concrete interests (the "objectives" of the planning) and means (the appropriation of the land). In Bilbao, the *Ensanches* created an entirely new city. If the old quarters of the *casco viejo* were on the right bank of the river, the *Ensanche* would extend the new city to the left bank, requiring the annexation of Abando's 158 hectares. The bridge of El Arenal served as the hinge linking the old and new cities.

The *Ensanche* marked the end of the closed urban structure which, on the one hand, was limited by the river and by the land of Abando, but, more importantly, was organized around a center (the elliptical plaza) and along a longitudinal axis (la Gran Vía). The two avenues of Mazarredo and Urquijo turned the *Ensanche* into an ellipse. The streets of Recalde, Elcano, and Ercilla were laid out as radii springing from the center. (See map at the end of this chapter.)

A debate that took place between the traditional sector (in favor of preserving the old quarters) and the modernizing sector in favor of the *Ensanche* revealed the conflicting nature of the rural and fishing interests on the one hand, and the industrial and mercantile ones on the other. Between 1857 and 1887 immigration to the mining and steel factories on the left bank tripled the population of towns such as *Baracaldo, Portugalete, and Santurce.* This demographic explosion forced the new laborers into hard living conditions in rooms next to their factory workplaces.

THE NERVIÓN, with its cheap and accessible transportation, became ever more central to the city's industrial resurgence. The ten miles on the left bank, from Bilbao to the seacoast, provided the best lands of the valley for all the heavy industries and proletarian housing. The right bank became residential, and except for the suspension bridge of Portugalete, until recently there were no bridges between the two banks.

The *Ensanche* became the controlling center of Bilbao's economic activities. The financial institutions moved there, and the houses of the elite were built in close proximity to the decision-making centers. Further enlargements to the Ensanche would eventually be necessary. The initial plans predicted 70,543 residents by 1924. The reality was that by 1920 the population was already 117,122 and by 1924, with the further annexation of Deusto, 140,722. The housing problem generated by Bilbao's industrial growth and immigration could not be resolved within the tightly structured and well-guarded Ensanche. In 1915 the population density of the lower class San Francisco district was 1,385 per hectare, but the Gran Vía, occupied in its initial blocks largely by banks, was only 190 per hectare. By then, two-thirds of Bilbao's population growth had been absorbed by its traditional quarters, not by the Ensanche.

IN 1800, ENGLAND had 9 million people, Germany 24 million, France 27 million, and the United States 5 million, and by 1930 the respective numbers were 45, 66, 42, and 130 million. Almost 80 percent of them were living in towns with populations higher than 2,500. Bilbao at the turn of the century, reshaped by immigration to work the mines and factories on the left bank, displayed some of the chaotic qualities described by Lewis Mumford in his "The Insensate Industrial Town." The traditional guilds were abolished, an open market for labor and for sale of goods was established, and foreign dependency for capital and raw materials was maintained. The economic foundations were the mines, the vastly increased production of iron, and the use of the steam engine. The myth of the untrammeled, unfettered lone individual was widely promulgated, and the overriding motif was human displacement.

Mechanization led to new levels of destruction to the environment and exhaustion of natural resources. Entire forests were razed, mountains leveled, and species driven to extinction. Nature was ruthlessly exploited in the name of profit. The ravaging of the environment reached its worst point in England around 1840. The devastation of the left bank of the Nervión River is another compelling testament to the ravages of industrialization.

The central economic ideology was utilitarian laissez-faire—industry should be self-regulated and government reduced to a minimum. The maximum good would come through the unregulated, self-aggrandizing efforts of every individual. With pecuniary reward the only measure of social value, and with profit the only controlling agent, gross social inequalities took root.

The techniques of agglomeration spanned all sectors of working life, from waterpower for the English factory system, to Watt's steam engine and the railroad transportation system. Port cities, such as Bilbao, termini of the main transportation lines, played an crucial role in the transformations. Bilbao became in effect an appendage of the British economic system. Population grew in the mining areas and along the new railroad lines. Since cities had labor supplies, they ipso facto became great industrial centers, which further stimulated urban growth and congestion.

The factory and the slum were the two main elements of the new urban complex. The factory was the nucleus of the urban organism, to which everything else was subordinate. It claimed the best placed sites, such as Bilbao's left bank. Waterfronts, rivers, and canals were offered up to industry, which used them as convenient dumping grounds, turning many of them into open sewers. Those who complained of dirt, noise, and so on were labeled effeminate, and Bilbao became the quintessential "tough city" (see chapter nineteen). The one-family-per-room "home" became standard from Dublin to Glasgow, from Bombay to Bilbao.

Lesson four

REQUIRED READING

Izaskun Echaniz, "Bilbao's Demographic and Urban Transformations" (portions of Chapter 2 from her Master's thesis, "The Social Consequences of Deindustrialization and Economic Regeneration in Bilbao: The Challenge of Urban Renewal").

SUGGESTED READING

Lewis Mumford, "The Insensate Industrial Town" (Chapter 3, The Culture of Cities, Harcourt, Brace & Co., New York, 1938).

LEARNING GOALS

1. Appreciate the relationship between industrialization, demographic growth, and urban structure.
2. Learn the transformations entailed from the old quarters to the new city of the Ensanche.
3. Understand the closed urban design and social structure of the Ensanche.
4. Identify Bilbao's historic role in experimenting with urban transformations to match the changing economic and demographic circumstances.

WRITTEN LESSON FOR SUBMISSION

Please write a two- to three-page essay on one of the topics below.

1. Describe the urban layout of Bilbao's Ensanche.
2. Which economic and social forces required this reinvention of Bilbao?
3. Discuss the interrelationship between the city's urban expression and its economic elite.
4. Do you recognize some of Mumford's "insensate industrial town" qualities in Bilbao? Explain.

5 · Traditional and metropolitan cultures

CONTEMPORARY CULTURE and avant-garde movements in the arts have been decisively influenced by the emergence of the twentieth-century metropolis. As examined by Raymond Williams, opportunities provided by the growth of cities promoted painting, sculpture, theater, and writing. The intellectual hegemony of the metropolitan centers were underscored by the fact that the major newspapers, magazines, publishing houses, museums, and galleries were located there. The rising culture was based on tenets that came to be called "modernist." Essential to such modernism were a set of aesthetic and intellectual "universals" based on the defined universality of a permanent human condition resistant to historical change or cultural diversity. Such modernist universals have recently come under criticism from postmodernist, postcolonialist, and feminist schools of thought. The metropolitan interpretation of its own cultural processes as timeless universals has been thoroughly brought into question.

The key cultural factor in the modernist shift was the character of the metropolis. Its most important element was immigration to the metropolitan industrial centers, manifested in art and culture by the themes of the city as a crowd of strangers, the individual's alienation, and the "impenetrability" of the city, in contrast to its vitality, variety, liberating mobility and seemingly endless sense of possibility. In the melting pot of the metropolis, individuals were forced to break apart from their traditional national cultures, and their actual community proved to be a community of occupational and urban practices. The social form of the metropolis is key to

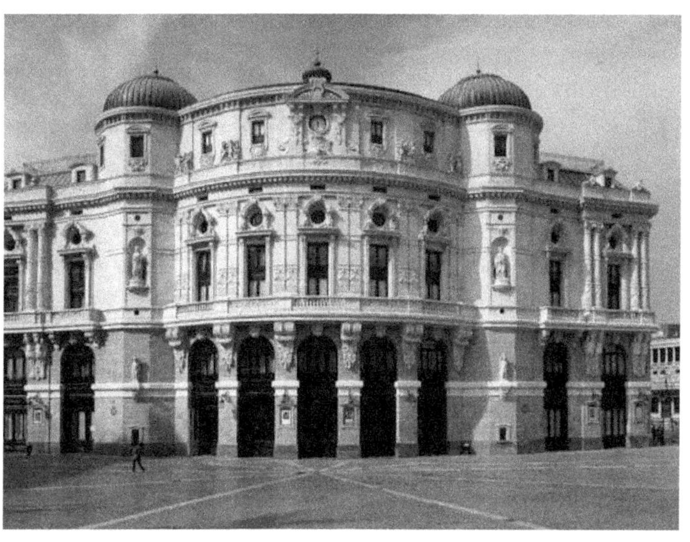

The Arriaga Theater, by architect Joaquin de Rucoba, was completed in 1890. It was a concert hall, restaurant, and a symbol of Bilbao's new cultural and industrial elite.
Photo: José Alberto Gandía.

understanding the new cultural institutions of art, museums, and journalism.

Language itself was perceived differently in the new setting. It was no longer customary and natural, but increasingly arbitrary and conventional. A new consciousness of changeable and open conventions emerged, and the metropolis created new visual and linguistic forms in its own right. In order to study Bilbao's entrepreneurial and metropolitan culture, Glass pays special attention to family, religion, education, wealth, and lifestyle. He compares Bilbao to Max Weber's famous thesis on the connection between Protestantism and capitalist development. He takes into account as well Arno Mayer's study of the persistence of aristocratic hegemony in European history.

BLASCO IBÁÑEZ'S novel, *El intruso*, reflects some of the essential tensions between traditional and modernist cultures, religion and science, and nationalism and socialism at the beginning of the twentieth century. It is a primary source for understanding the transformations in Basque traditional society, confronted with the new cultures of the working classes, industrialization, capitalism, and irreligiosity. In an exaggerated manner, the anticlerical Ibáñez portrays the pernicious effects of religion on Bilbao's life, exemplified by the intrusion of priests into the households of wealthy businessmen by playing on the spiritual cravings of their wives.

Business and piety complement each another in the traditional Basque work ethic. The many religious fraternities, dating back to the sixteenth century, testify to the religious convictions of Basque entrepeneurs. The ninteenth-century Bilbao business elite displayed the same combination of piety and industry. For example, the mines were named after saints, and prominent businessmen had private chapels in their homes. Many of their children became nuns and priests. The nun Rafaela Ybarra, of the wealthy Ybarra family, was beatified. The wills of large merchants often contained requests to be buried wearing the habit of their religious orders.

The University of Deusto was founded in 1883 by Bilbao's various prominent business leaders and operated by the Jesuits. It became the educational center of the industrial city's new elites. The University of Deusto's Business School, founded in 1916, was the first university in Spain dedicated to the study of economics. Catholicism was the paramount teaching in this Jesuit university. The piety of Vizcayan entrepeneurs, coexisting with a long tradition of capitalist enterprise, is a result of the influence of their strong religious education, defying Weber's thesis that Calvinism was a central condition for the rise of European capitalism.

IN CONTRAST TO Blasco Ibáñez's unflattering portrait of the intrusive Jesuits, they had been supporters the entrepeneurial spirit of the middle classes since the eighteenth century, extolling work and discipline, praising the virtues of work over aristocratic values, and arguing that merchants were not thieves. Even Unamuno criticized the Jesuits for fostering such entrepeneurial-friendly education. The Jesuits believed in sanctifying the lay life just as much as the Calvinists did. There was no greater praise than industriousness and no greater dishonors than laziness and begging. This pro-business mentality was supported by social ideologies, family structures, and ethnic solidarity.

The significance of large families in promoting successful business networks cannot be overstated. It is illustrated by the prominent Vizcayan families, such as the Ybarras and the Sotas. Family continuity within the business elite was not so much a question of generational sequence as of the interplay of personal aspirations, socioeconomic climate, and political circumstances. Marriage partners had to be carefully selected and marriages were usually arranged by parents. Although not rigidly endogamous, the Vizcayan aristocratic families, with few exceptions, employed marriage to consolidate their economic position.

Manuel Basas concluded that many of Bilbao's millionaires had made their fortunes abroad. In fact, there is a vast Basque diaspora network dating back to the sixteenth century. Bilbao's metropolitan culture was significantly shaped by these integral foreign connections. Bilbao's literacy rate was close to the highest in Spain. Its merchants would send their sons to England, France, Germany, or Belgium to be educated and to learn foreign languages. Such opportunities were crucial to the evolution of family businesses from commerce to industry (engineering and law were the most popular fields of study). Inventions such as the Bessemer converter impressed local entrepreneurs with the significance of technical knowledge. Education was clearly more than a matter of prestige: it was necessary to provide the practical skill to operate the factories.

HISTORIAN MANUEL Tuñón de Lara argued that the main feature of nineteenth century Spanish history was the integration of nobility and the upper middle class. In this view, the aristocracy imposed its cultural values on a mesmerized bourgeoisie. Arno Mayer makes the same argument. Many of Bilbao's business elite families (the Aznars, Ybarras, Sotas, MacMahons, Villalongas, Zubirias, among others) were granted titles of nobility during the 1890s and early 1900s. Although this would seem to demonstrate a disposition to seeking honor and status, Glass argues that it nonetheless does not necessarily indicate a betrayal of bourgeois values. The aristocratic mentality of inherited privileges did not override the sense of the value of personal accomplishment for Vizcayan businessmen. They would lecture their sons, for example, that obtaining a university degree was more important than possessing a noble title. Ennobled businessmen lived little-changed lives before and after receiving the honor.

The consumption patterns of the business elite are revealing of their cultural values. A study of twenty-one cases shows that the spending on "furniture, jewelry, and clothing," accounted for only 1.2 percent of their total expenditures. (In Paris such expenditures accounted for 2.25 percent for the same period). Bilbao business elites lived rather modestly compared with the rich Madrid financiers. Bilbao had only one theater where popular operas and plays were staged during a six-month annual season. The church considered the theater morally ambiguous. Stern puritanism characterized the bourgeois classes. Music was nonetheless passionately enjoyed, although elaborate balls were virtually unknown, and to this day a vibrant musical tradition survives in Bilbao.

During the 1880s and 1890s elite families began to build mansions in new neighborhoods such as Abando and Deusto. Some moved a few miles from Bilbao to Las Arenas and Neguri, which were turned into upper-class residential areas. Glamorous leisure activities, such as yachting, became popular. The Spanish King Alfonso XIII frequently presided over the summer sporting events, such as the regattas. In addition to Bilbaina, the traditional recreational center for the elite, new clubs, such as the Real Sporting Club and the Club Maritimo were organized. These centers and associated activities served as meeting places for the elites, and provided opportunities to lobby government ministers in social circumstances.

GLASS CONCLUDES that the Basque case presents a glaring counterexample to Weber's thesis. Under the influence of the Jesuits, the devout Vizcayan businessmen displayed traits similar to those ascribed to the Calvinists by Weber. Their work ethic was complemented by family networks at home and abroad, by a cosmopolitanism which kept them abreast of new technologies, and by the education their sons abroad, all of which facilitated the importation of new ideas and skills. Hard work, personal merit, education, and a disposition to invest rather than consume were the formative bourgeois values of Bilbao's business elite.

Lesson five

REQUIRED READING

Eduardo Glass, "Business, Culture, and Society" (Chapter 5, Bilbao's Modern Business Elite, Univ. of Nevada, Reno, 1997).

SUGGESTED READING

Raymond Williams, "Metropolitan Perceptions and the Emergence of Modernism" (The Politics of Modernism, Verso, London, 1989).

LEARNING GOALS

1. Understand the relationship between modernism and the urban metropolis.
2. Identify the dynamics of traditional and metropolitan cultures in Bilbao.
3. Explore the lifestyle of Bilbao's modern business elite.

WRITTEN LESSON FOR SUBMISSION

Please write a two- to three-page essay on one of the topics below.

1. Does Bilbao offer a counterexample to Weber's thesis on the connection between Protestantism and capitalist development?

2. Describe the influence of religion on Basque businessmen.
3. Does Bilbao's business elite display aristocratic or bourgeois values? What are these basic values?
4. Do you see early twentieth-century Bilbao as a fully metropolitan modernist culture? Provide examples.

6 · That old Bilbao moon

Race, sexuality, and myth

Bilbao Song
Bill's dancehall in Bilbao, Bilbao, Bilbao
Was the most beautiful on the whole continent
There for one dollar you could get noise and pleasure, noise and pleasure, noise and pleasure
And what the world calls its own.
But if you would have walked in there
I'm not sure whether you care for that sort of thing:
There was brandy and laughter wherever you sat
And the grass grew through the dance floor
And the green moon shone through the roof.
The music there—they really gave you your money's worth!

Joe, play that old music
That old Bilbao moon
There love was worthwhile!
That old Bilbao moon
He was used to Brazilian cigars
That old Bilbao moon
I've said it often
That old Bilbao moon
He never held me down
I'm not so sure you would have liked it—still
It was the most beautiful!
It was the most beautiful!
It was the most beautiful
In the world!

Bill's dancehall in Bilbao, Bilbao, Bilbao
On a day in May in '08
There came from Frisco four guys with gold bags,

Gold bags, gold bags,
And they did something with us then!
If you would have been there
I'm not sure at all whether you would have cared for that sort of thing.
Oh, there was brandy laughter wherever you sat
And grass grew though the dance floor
And the green moon shone through the roof.
And you could hear the four guys popping off their pistols.
Are you a hero?
Well, try and do the same!
That old Bilbao moon
There where love was worthwhile!

That old Bilbao moon
He was used to Brazilian cigars
That old Bilbao moon
I've said it often
That old Bilbao moon
He never held me down
I'm not so sure you would have liked it—still
It was the most beautiful!
It was the most beautiful!
It was the most beautiful
In the world!

Bill's dancehall in Bilbao, Bilbao, Bilbao
Now it's renovated and very phony
With palms and ice cream—very ordinary, very ordinary, very ordinary.
Just like any other establishment.
If you would sail in this very moment
It's quite possible you would like it
Unfortunately I have no fun with that

No grass is growing through the dance floor
And the green moon has been cancelled.
The kind of music they play there now
—you'd be ashamed of it
Joe, play that old-time music
That old Bilbao moon
Oh, how did it go?
He used to smoke Brazilian cigars
Oh, I've forgotten the words.
There where love still dwells
It's been so long ago
I'm not so sure you would have liked it—still
It was the most beautiful!
It was the most beautiful!
It was the most beautiful
In the world!

Brecht and Weill's world-renowned "Bilbao Song" gives a taste of the mythology of a city. It was originally performed by Lotte Lenya, and more recently by solo singers such as Ute Lumper and Marianne Faithful and jazz groups such as Gil Evans and Clusone.

William Blake's London, Baudelaire's Paris, and Joyce's turn-of-the-century Dublin are good illustrations of "imaginary cities" that have left their marks on the cultures of their times. Walter Benjamin's arcade project presents a classical example of how to study such urban phantasmagoria.

THOUGH BRECHT apparently never actually visited Bilbao he perfectly captured the ethos of a European port city, right down to its thriving red light district (located next to the mining neighborhood in *Bilbao la Vieja* or "Old Bilbao") frequented by workers, seamen, and a wide variety of the city's residents. In the previous chapter we insisted on the religious components of

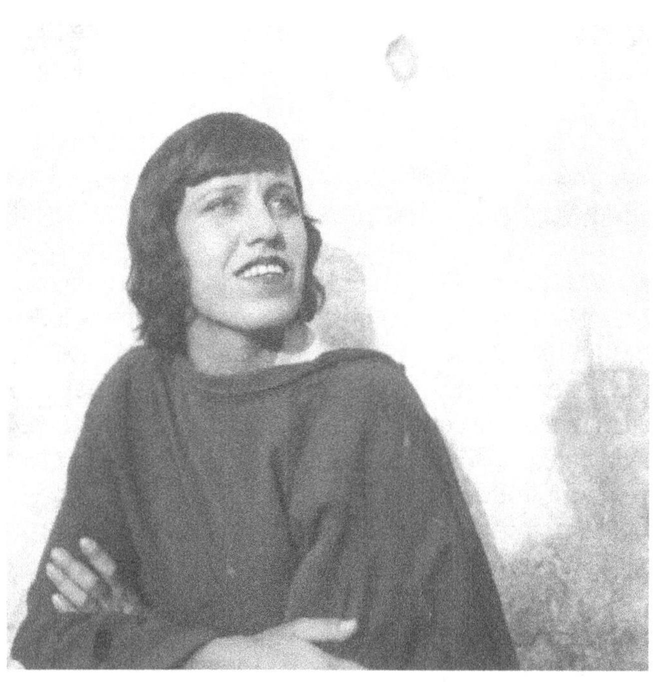

The incomparable Lotte Lenya in the nineteen-twenties. *Photo courtesy of the Kurt Weill Foundation for Music, New York.*

Bilbao's urban and entrepreneurial culture, but this does not preclude us from paying attention to the more phantasmagoric realities of myth, sex and even race.

Carl Schorske's article and the chapters on industrialization and metropolitan culture provide an overall perspective of "the city as virtue." A second major theme of the city in European intellectual history is "the city as vice." Blasco Ibáñez's *El intruso* stages, in dramatic terms, the fight between virtue and vice in the religious climate of industrial Bilbao. The fallen view of the city is symbolized in the grime and squalor of industrialism, urban decay, and prostitution. Whether socialists or nationalists, philosophers or ethnographers, historians or poets, Bilbaino writers have been unanimous in their disapproval of the social and moral ills of their city. For them the city as vice has been a permanent topic. Socialists lash out at unjust working conditions and to promote a utopian view of the future. Nationalists lament the ills brought about by non-Basque and nonreligious immigrants working in Bilbao's mines and factories, while fostering a nostalgic view of the preindustrial, preurban Basque country.

IF ONE REACTION to the grime and corruption of industrial Bilbao was nostalgia for the archaic "purity" of former agrarian life, the opposite reaction was the futurism of social reformers inspired by the ideals of the Enlightenment. Side by side with the prophetic vision of Christianity and, conversely, violently opposed to it, the other major influence was the revolutionary ideology of Marxism. As Marx rejected capitalism for its exploitation of the workers, Engels rejected the industrial city as the site of labor oppression and future theater of proletarian revolution. Blasco Ibáñez's novel, emulating Zola's work across the Pyrenees, expressed this view perfectly. The cures would come not from religion, but from the metropolis itself, and its capacity for fostering scientific advancement and civic culture. The very forces of ugly repression would turn into the forces of secular redemption.

At the turn of the century, Bilbao's artists were visiting Paris, the European artistic mecca. A new mode of thinking and feeling had emerged there, centered on the work of impressionist painters and writers such as

Baudelaire. With Nietzsche providing the philosophical formulation, the movement explicitly challenged traditional morality and art. Personal experience was pronounced the only valid arbiter. Morality and art were deemed to be beyond good and evil. As was the idea of the city itself.

WHAT WAS GOOD or bad about modern life was no longer at stake, just how to experience life fully. The city became the explicit ground of modern existence. Though it was the site of the cataclysmic changes celebrated by modernity, it provided a firm background; the *site* of the transience remained the same. For the Basques, Bilbao was that site. Only Bilbao, with its port and industries, its great eclectic architecture and urban life, its shopping districts, and cabaret life in the red light district, had the necessary spirit of vitality of a modern city. We don't think of a city in isolation, but through our own inherited culture and personal experience. If the poet Rilke thought of the city as collective fatality, these new fatalists would find beauty in urban degradation itself. All the city has to offer might be the Baudelairian "flowers of evil," but flowers are still flowers; even Rimbaud's secular illuminations become possible there. The new poetry of the urban spirit emphasized the aesthetic power of the individual in the face of fate. Bilbao's aesthetics of "tough city," celebrated by Frank Gehry and Richard Serra, share the view that urban ruins and degradation can themselves provide the ground for beauty.

Bilbao was also the site of Basque nationalist politics, whose avowed goals were the preservation of the local pre-Indo-European language and culture. Basque traditional ethnographic culture was heavily racialized by European anthropology. The mythified role played by Basques in academic representations is that of an original enclave of non-Indo-European stock, not only in linguistic terms, but in racial ones as well. Unfortunately, Basque nationalism relied on such academic representations. The article I wrote with William Douglass examines and debunks the conceptual bases of such racial formations.

The new modernist perspectives arising from deracinated city experience could not be more removed from the roots of ethnographic culture and racialist politics. Bilbao was a political and cultural battleground for the working out of such starkly contrasting viewpoints. The present urban transformation of Bilbao replays these battles with ongoing dialectics between the local and the global, the roots and the routes, exacerbated by the exaggerated claims of each side in the debate.

BOTH SAN SEBASTIÁN and Bilbao have played out their collective representations in quite different registers. San Sebastián, with clear French *Belle Epoque* and Art Deco influences in its architecture, has projected itself as a small bourgeois spa city ideal for tourism and summer vacationing. Bilbao is thought to be a much larger city, the capital of Basque finances and heavy industries, proud of its commercial and industrial history. The differences between the two cities are depicted almost in female / male terms, the local community versus the industrial metropolis. The reality is that the demographic differences (Bilbao with a population of 350,000; San Sebastián, 180,000; Vitoria has 210,000) and economic differences between the Basque provincial capitals are not that great. However, Bilbao has proven best able to project strong, modernist images such as "metropolitan Bilbao" or "the great Bilbao," by concentrating mining, industry, shipping, and banking in a single urban productive area. With close to one million residents, nearly half the population of the Basque autonomous region resides in greater Bilbao.

It should be emphasized, as pointed out by Arpal, that the city itself becomes the most significant representation of modern society. It organizes space, time, and urbanism. In the Basque case, the representational differences between Bilbao as the tough industrial city, San Sebastián as the pretty beach resort city, and Vitoria-Gasteiz as the administrative center have served to articulate a series of collective images. Critical differences regarding the economic crisis of the 1980s, the political redefining of the role of provincial capital in the autonomous community of the Basque country, and the accessibility of public funds for each city's urban regeneration projects are played out in such competitive contexts. The fact that Bilbao is now projecting itself as a music and tourist center is a clear emblem of the vast transformations in basic Basque economic structure.

Lesson six

REQUIRED READING

Jesus Arpal, "Cities in the Basque Country: An Area of Collective Representation" (in Urban Transformations: Projects and Lectures, Gipuzkoako Foru Aldundia, Donostia, 1994).

SUGGESTED READING

Bertolt Brecht, "Bilbao Song," as performed by Marianne Faithfull on Seven Deadly Sins" BMG Classics, 1998.

Carl Schorske, "The Idea of the City in European Thought" (in Sylvia Fleiss, ed., Urbanism in World

Perspective: A Reader, Thomas Y. Cromwell Co., New York, 1968).

W. Douglass and J. Zulaika, "Creating the Basque Race."

LEARNING GOALS

1. Be able to interpret cities as purely imaginary constructs, as well as the sites of modern dwelling.
2. Assess the significance of visual and written arts in the mythification of cities.
3. Pay attention to Bilbao's cabaret culture as a prelude to the urban transformations stimulated by the Guggenheim Effect.
4. Learn about the inherent tensions between ethnographic and modernist representations of the Basques.

WRITTEN LESSON FOR SUBMISSION

Please write a two- to three-page essay on one of the topics below.

1. Comment on Brecht's "Bilbao Song." What does it reflect, and achieve by evoking "that old Bilbao moon"?
2. Elaborate on the implications of interpreting Bilbao along the lines of Schorske's "city as vice."
3. Discuss the differences and similarities between the archaic and utopian solutions to the ills of industrial life.
4. Describe the recent transformations in the relationships between the Basque provincial capitals and what those changes reflect.

7 · The rise and fall of the industrial model

THE TRANSFORMATION OF Bilbao turned the Basque region into a heavily industrialized society. By 1955, 44 percent of Basques worked in industry, while the countrywide average was only 29 percent. In 1960, 46.3 percent worked in industry (higher than the average throughout the European Common Market), and overall 52.3 percent of the population were employed in industry-related work. In 1960 the per capita income of Basques was 70 percent higher than the Spanish-wide average. Among the fifty Spanish provinces, Vizcaya, Gipuzkoa, Araba, and Navarra were respectively first, second, third, and ninth in income aver-age. After 1960 a rapid economic and demographic expansion took place and the annual growth of the gross national product was estimated to be 7.7 per-cent, with the growth of the industrial national product of the Basques estimated at 10.1 (similar to Spain but double that of major western economies).

The basic institutional features of the Spanish economy at the time were protectionism for the interior market, national planning (which favored investments in certain sectors and regions), an abundance of cheap labor from rural areas, and specialization in industries with high energy costs. These features led to a pattern of development that lacked innovative stimuli, in its productive and organizational aspects and in commercial aspects, and that ultimately failed to produce exportable commodities.

Differential aspects of the Basque economy within the Spanish economy were: specialization of a relative few sectors; an emphasis on the basic sectors of metallurgy; and continued large immigration from the rest of Spain.

Breakdown by sector of the European workforce for the years 1960 and 1975:

	Agriculture		**Industry**		**Services**	
	1960	**1975**	**1960**	**1975**	**1960**	**1975**
Germany	13.8	7.4	48.2	46.0	38.0	46.6
France	22.4	11.3	39.0	38.6	38.5	50.0
CEE-9*	17.2	8.7	43.3	41.7	39.5	49.7
Spain	40.5	22.9	30.3	36.8	29.2	40.3
Basque C.	21.5	10.7	46.3	52.9	32.2	36.4

**The nine countries of the European Common Market.*

The productive sectors in the Basque Country from 1960 to 1975 were mining (1.2 percent), construction (5.1 percent), water, gas, and electricity (2.4 percent), food and drink (3.9 percent), textiles (1.7 percent), manufacturing and footwear (1.6 percent), wood (2.3 percent), paper (3.1 percent), chemicals (7.5 percent), cement, ceramics, and glass (1.3 percent), metallurgic industries (22.2 percent), agriculture (10.9 percent), fishing (2.4 percent), transportation and communication (5.6 percent), commerce (8.6 percent), finance and banking (2.1 percent), housing (4.6 percent), public administration (3.2 percent), and other sectors (10.7 percent). Between 1955 and 1973 Bilbao led the Basque economy with the creation of 250,000 new jobs (enlarging the number of positions by 34 percent increase over the 1955 workforce). Seven out of ten new jobs were in industry, which grew at an annual 7.1 percent rate, while the services sector grew at a rate of only 4.2 percent. In

1975, 52.9 percent of the total Basque work force was in industry and construction work (the figure for 1960 was 46.3 percent), while throughout the European Economic Community that sector was shrinking from 43.3 percent (1960) to 41.7 percent (1975).

BETWEEN 1950 AND 1975, the population increased by 1,112,000, bringing the total population to 2,556,000 (a 77 percent increase over 1950). During the first half of the twentieth century, the annual population growth was 0.93 percent; from 1950 to 1975 it was 2.31 percent, notably larger than the rest of Spain (annual average of 1.01 percent) and the EEC (0.72 percent). Direct migration to the Basque country between 1950 and 1975 was 387,000 (35 percent of the population increase), but when the higher reproduction the high rates of the immigrants are factored in, the percentage rises to 53.

This heavily industrialized economic model could not be maintained. The Basque economy was severely affected by the international economic crisis of the late 1970s. Due to its small size and heavy industrialization with little diversification, the Basque economy was highly dependent on external factors. In 1974 and 1975 the industrial growth of the European countries was respectively 0.8 percent and –4.6 percent, but until 1977, Basque industry continued to increase at a 4 percent annual rate. In 1977 the economic crisis set in full force, resulting in a reduction of the National Economic Product (NEP), a drastic fall in investments, and a significant rise in unemployment due to factory closings in several industries. A change in the structure of production took place and between 1977 and 1981 and there was a significant reduction in the annual NEP (–2.1). Recovery was slower than the rest of Spain, but between 1981 and 1985 the NEP enjoyed a 1.2 percent increase. In 1975 Vizcaya and Gipuzkoa were respectively first and third among the Spanish provinces in per capita growth, but by 1985 they had dropped to fourteenth and eleventh.

Structural changes also occurred. The industry sector shrank from 47.9 percent of the Basque economy in 1972 to 41.8 percent in 1985. At the same time the service sector grew from 43.1 percent in 1972 to 50.3 percent in 1985. Finally, after 1981, investments improved due to the improved international situation, a better benefit ratio for enterprises, the recovery of the NEP, the lowering of interest rates, the consolidation of democracy, public financing of horizontal investment, sectorial plans for reconversion, and Spain's entrance into the EEC.

Comparative percentage participation of the first six sectors of the industrial investment in Spain and the Basque country:

	Basque Country 1982–1986*	**Spain 1981–1985***
Steel and iron	28.7	7.7
Food, drink and tobacco	9.5	18.9
Tools and metallurgic products	8.7	5.2
Paper	5.7	4.2
Electronic/electronic materials	5.6	5.6
Automobiles	4.1	10.5

**construction excluded*

Unemployment was the main sign of the severity of the economic crisis, particularly among youth and women. Between 1973 and 1985 194,000 jobs were lost in the Basque economy. Still, this was a smaller number than in 1960, when the population was 900,000 greater. In 1986 unemployment in the Basque region was 23.1 percent, compared with Spain at 21.5 percent and European countries at 10 percent. During most of the 1990s unemployment was over 20 percent, with Bilbao in the lead. From 1975 to 1987 there was a drastic drop in the Bilbao population rate of increase: the birthrate began to decline, and a negative migration began in 1977.

In conclusion, by the middle 1980s there was a clear exhaustion of the previous model of development imposed by Bilbao's industrial history. Structural changes were necessary to insulate the Basque economy from international crises. Industry still played too dominant a role, and inefficient new investments returned to low profits in the face of great technological changes. There was little research and technological innovation, and high rates of unemployment.

AFTER 1985 THERE was an economic recovery of sorts, though not a very harmonious one. The Basque economy remained highly dependent on the global economy, because it specialized in sectors that produce for export. (Although its "natural" market expanded greatly with its entrance into the EEC, 350 million people large.) Technological obsolescence was dealt with by creating new technology parks next to the three provincial capitals of Bilbao, San Sebastián, and Vitoria. The region had become a zone of industrial decline where it was increasingly difficult to woo foreign investment. In 1993 the unemployment rate was still 21.4 percent, and of the 36,000 jobs lost in 1992, 20,000 were in the no-longer-competitive industrial sector.

But if the present difficulties can be surmounted, the Basque region will have, overall, fared well through its period of intense industrialization. In 1960, Bilbao's per capita income was $1,000; in 1993 it was $14,500, 83 percent of the European average.

Lesson seven

REQUIRED READING

Eduardo Glass, "Conclusion" (Chapter 7, Bilbao's Modern Business Elite, Univ. of Nevada, Reno, 1997).

Izaskun Echaniz, "The De-industrialization Process in Bilbao" (Chapter 3, Master's Thesis, The Social Consequences of De-industrialization in Bilbao: The Challenge of Urban Renewal).

LEARNING GOALS

1. Identify the elements that made Bilbao's industrial model so successful.
2. Understand the vulnerabilities of this industrial model.
3. Identify the elements that precipitated Bilbao's demise.
4. Learn about Bilbao's deindustrialization process.

WRITTEN LESSON FOR SUBMISSION

Please write a two- to three-page essay on one of the topics below.

1. What are, according to Glass, the basic components of Bilbao's successful industrial model?
2. Examine the links between Glass's industrial model and Bilbao's economic boom of the 1950s and 1960s and its bust of the 1970s and 1980s.

3. Provide some basic employment, migration and economic figures as evidence of Bilbao's deindustrialization process.
4. What are the lessons to be learned and challenges presented by Bilbao's experience with industrialization?

8 · Necessary ruins

Walter Benjamin wrote:

A Klee painting named "Angelus Novus" shows an angel looking as though he is about to move away from something he is fixedly contemplating. His eyes are staring, his mouth is open, his wings are spread. This is how one pictures the angel of history. His face is turned toward the past. Where we perceive a chain of events, he sees one single catastrophe which keeps piling wreckage upon wreckage and hurls it in front of his feet. The angel would like to stay, awaken the dead, and make whole what has been smashed. But a storm is blowing from Paradise; it has got caught in his wings with such violence that the angel can no longer close them. This storm irresistibly propels him into the future to which his back is turned, while the pile of debris before him grows skyward. This storm is what we call progress. (Thesis IX)

HISTORY IS A PROCESS of decay and ruin—this is the quintessential perspective that emerges from Bilbao's *fin de millennium*. Were it not for the spectacular ruins of its metropolitan area, Bilbao would be a typical European provincial city exuding a bourgeois lifestyle. The aesthetics of the "tough city" set Bilbao apart.

The industrial and urban wasteland of Bilbao's left bank is made up of kilometers of ruins, hundreds of buildings silently awaiting demolition, urban neighborhoods with deserted streets, industrial sites with dormant chimneys, entire valleys awash in pollution, a river bank contaminated beyond redemption, residential zones and garden areas adjacent to the most devastated

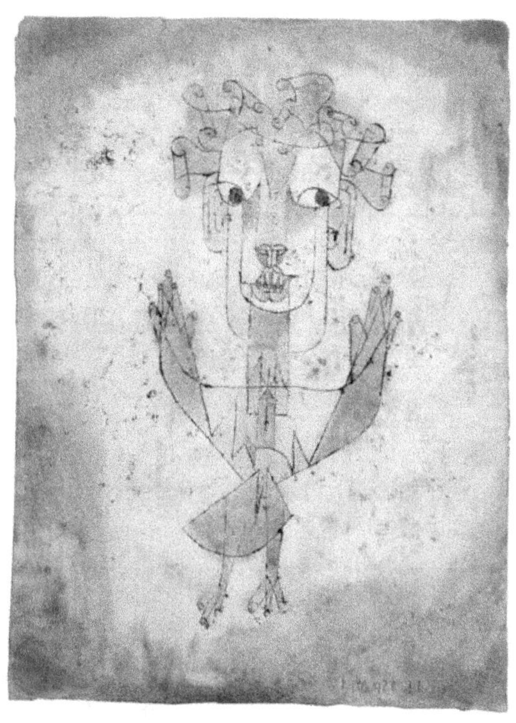

Paul Klee's Angelus Novus (1920) is a modest work. It was drawn on paper in India ink and color chalks, followed by a brown wash.
Photo: Israel Museum, Jerusalem.

---

areas. By 1995, *Altos Hornos de Vizcaya*, the smoky "tall ovens" of fire that supported tens of thousands of families, the blast furnaces that were the proud emblem of the left bank's vast industrial complex, had shut down. In the municipal area of Bilbao alone there are 52 industrial ruins occupying 48 hectares of land. Baracaldo, the next town on the left bank, has another 25 industrial ruins occupying 100 hectares. One-third of Sestao, the next municipality, is in ruins. The bookstores of Bilbao prominently feature photo reports chronicling the demolition of the city's disused factories.

METROPOLITAN BILBAO also contains about 9 million square meters of contaminated land. There are 135 industrial dumps and twenty sites that are contaminated with lindane, a highly toxic pesticide. One factory in Baracaldo has 4,500 tons of lindane in its pure state. Another 80,000 tons of lindane is mixed with the soil and is the legacy of defunct chemical factories. It is estimated that there is a total of 300,000 cubic meters of lindane contaminating the region.

But ruins beckon new architecture, new beginnings, in a new millennia, and Bilbao is poised to produce them in abundance. In the beginning there were only ruins, but now there is Gehry's Bilbao Guggenheim Museum, Foster's underground metro, and soon, the Abandoibarra redevelopment project. The staggering ruins of the Nervión's left bank justify for some the dominance of the architectural star system in Bilbao. The danger seen by others is the imposition of a dazzling architectural motif that becomes a new authoritarian master, a narcissistic trap that turns citizens into voyeurs of their politicians' grandiose projects. Cultural objectives and economic needs may prove secondary to the architectonic vision.

Susan Buck-Morss has commented on Benjamin's perspective of history as a process of relentless disintegration, of which the Bilbao ruins are emblematic. Benjamin learned from the Baroque poets that the failed materials of their own period could be elevated to allegory. What made this so valuable for him was that, in a dialectical demonstration of modernity, allegory and myth had become antithetical, that is, allegory was proving to be the antidote to a mythic view of historical progress. He established a parallel between ruins and allegories in which "allegory is in the realm of thought what ruins are in the realm of things."

Benjamin thought that allegory was as valid as symbol (see chapter twenty-eight, "Bilbao as Ruin, Architecture and Allegory"). In allegory, history appears as nature in decay or in a state of ruin, and the temporal mode is one of retrospective contemplation. In the symbol, time enters as the instantaneous present of the mystical now. In symbol, nature is bud and bloom, in allegory nature overripens and decays. Allegory becomes, for Benjamin, a cognitive imperative, since certain epochs and experiences are allegorical. Bilbao's *fin de millennium*, full of ruins and great architectural projects, is a cultural period of intensely allegorical nature.

BAUDELAIRE, WITH HIS poetic *Fleurs du mal* and his rage against the new urban phantasmagoria, was a hero to Benjamin. By providing a decadent sense of the modern city experience, his writing manifested a radically new aesthetic sensibility. The people who interested him were prostitutes, poor women, dying people, and night revelers. The prostitute presented the ur-form, the essential depiction, of the wage laborer, who was an objective emblem of capitalism, a dialectical image reflecting a synthesis of the form (seller) and content (body) of the commodity. He was concerned with the premodern Christian problems of sin and evil now expressed in allegorical form. By sustaining allegory he guaranteed the continuity of the literary tradition. Baudelaire emphasized the commodity in order to experience it from inside and assume its guilt as his own. He hated people's faith in progress and tried to destroy the harmonious façade of historical progression. In the end his rage turned into resignation, and he settled for holding onto the ruins. Benjamin criticizes him for ontologizing the emptiness of the historical experience of the commodity. Benjamin thought that the idea of history as catastrophe is still another myth, a child's kaleidoscope used to organize everything in a negative order, and it too must be analyzed critically.

Lesson eight

SUGGESTED READING

Walter Benjamin, "Theses on the Philosophy of History" (Illuminations, Harcourt, Brace and World, Inc., New York, 1968).

Susan Buck-Morss, "Historical Nature: Ruin" (in The Dialectics of Seeing: Walter Benjamin and the Arcades Project, MIT Press, Cambridge, 1989).

LEARNING GOALS

1. Foster a critical sense of the view of history as constant progress.
2. Apply the view of history as decay to Bilbao.
3. Call attention to Bilbao's ruins.
4. Establish conceptual links between ruins and allegories.

WRITTEN LESSON FOR SUBMISSION

Please write a two- to three-page essay on one of the topics below.

1. Describe the ruins of Bilbao. What do they represent?
2. "Allegory is in the realm of thought what ruins are in the realm of things." Comment.
3. In which sense are ruins "necessary"?
4. Associate economic, social, and cultural ruins. Provide examples from Bilbao.

9 · Gentrification

THE FUNDAMENTAL LOGIC of capital is one of devaluation and revaluation as a response to market forces. As ruination (previous chapter) has to do with the process of devaluation, gentrification (from "gentry") implies revaluation. The rent gap (the disparity between the actual ground rent value and the potential one) is the index that regulates this process. Gentrification takes place when the gap is large enough to provide a positive return to the developer after all the costs of building and loans have been paid. Gentrification can help entire neighborhoods begin a renewed life.

The ruins of the docks in Abandoibarra, the ecological devastation of the left bank of the river, and the derelict state of many neighborhoods offer opportunities for the gentrification of Bilbao. The relationship between the two processes is obvious if one simply steps from the glorious *Abandoibarra* (the site of the Guggenheim, the *Euskalduna* Convention Center, and Pelli's future center) to the adjacent ruin-strewn neighborhood of Zorrozaurre. Neighborhoods such as Bilbao La Vieja are illustrative of Bilbao's need for gentrification: they are very close to the city center, yet derelict, with several buildings already in a state of collapse.

It is commonplace to apply the imagery of urban wilderness and frontier to inner cities, where crime and drugs find refuge. Such "jungles" are described by means of the discourse of urban and social decline, and the loss of the historical and geographical qualities of specific places lends them to such mythification. This mythology prepares the ground for the sanitizing effects of gentrification. The depiction of urban life as a fable replete with dangers constitutes an entire cinematic genre. This ideological divide between the civil and uncivil neighborhoods is not entirely innocent, since it is used to rationalize the violence of the transformations gentrification brings about.

"Is gentrification a dirty word?" asked a full-sized *New York Times* ad paid for by the Real Estate Board of New York. "In simple terms, gentrification is the upgrading of housing and retail businesses in a neighborhood with an influx generally of *private* investment," explained the defensive ad. How did gentrification become such a contested issue? The term was coined by Ruth Glass in 1964, to describe how the working class quarters of London were invaded by the middle classes. "Shabby, modest mews and cottages—two rooms up and two down—have been taken over, when their leases have expired, and have become elegant, expensive residences." Once the process of gentrification begins in a district, it proceeds rapidly until "the whole social character of the district is changed."

IN THE PREVIOUS chapter on ruins we mentioned Baudelaire's rage against urban phantasmagoria. One of his contemporaries, Baron Haussmann, personifies gentrification. He was known for replacing the working class neighborhoods of Paris during the 1850s and 1860s with boulevards and monumental buildings. The term "Haussmannian" came to represent social control of the lower classes by means of urban "improvements" that simultaneously extol the "embourgeoisement" of the middle classes.

Gentrification has become a common phenomenon. Smith estimates that by 1976 nearly half of US cities with a population above 50,000 were experiencing gentrification. In fact, gentrification is undoubtedly the hallmark of the emerging global city. Its central meaning is

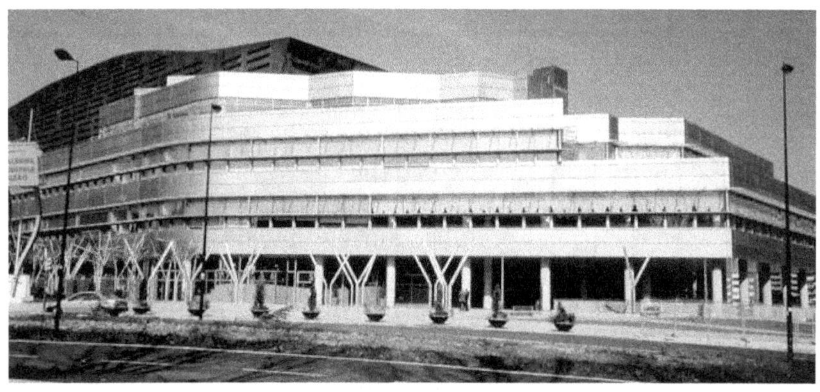

The Abandoibarra riverfront development will include a convention center and concert hall, *Euskalduna*, in the very place where men toiled in the Euskalduna shipyards for a hundred years.
Photo: Txetxu Berruezo and Josu Bilbao Fullaondo.

---

urban rehabilitation, but suburbanization and gentrification are closely connected.

The ruins of Bilbao beckon toward the promoters of gentrification and redevelopment. Bilbao had been a typical European bourgeois city providing the banking and commercial services to an industrial center. The closing of the heavy iron and steel industries, and the demise of the working classes that ran them, reinforced the class differences between the unemployed and early retired, and the middle classes. The "new" Bilbao, proud of its flagship developments, is a city intent in recreating a new urban landscape that will attract investors and tourists. Urban redevelopment by means of flagship projects symbolizes the political power to determine the future of the city.

BILBAO WAS THE birthplace of Basque and Spanish socialism at the turn of the nineteenth century, and a proud working class culture forms the center of Bilbao's industrial life. Labor unions, capable of organizing massive strikes, were powers to be reckoned with until the 1980s. The video on the battle of *Euskalduna* provides graphic testimony of the last working-class battle in the streets of Bilbao during the mid-1980s.

Bilbao illustrates the relationship between gentrification and globalization. The ruin of its iron and shipbuilding industries is directly related to processes of globalization. The consequence is the necessity of replacing the lost industries with a service and tourism economy. Via its symbiotic relationship to Great Britain, Bilbao, historically, has been at the core of the world capitalist system. Hit hard by the universalizing tendency of capital and its latest "shrinking of the world," Bilbao has been forced to look back at its history in order to regain self-confidence. Thus the rhythm of an urban economy is closely related to the rhythms of the national and international economy and crises are not accidental interruptions in an otherwise harmonious environment. There is a strong tendency for capital to undergo periodic and systematic changes when invested in the built environment. Gentrification is intimately tied to these larger processes, and Bilbao's ongoing renewal process is part of this historical pattern of investment and divestment.

Deindustrialization and ruination drive redevelopment and gentrification in a spatial restructuring of cities at the national and global levels. The logic of uneven development of capital becomes most glaring at the urban frontier. That is, the development of one area creates barriers to further development—in fact, underdeveloping and ruining them—thus creating opportunities for a new phase of development. Gentrification and redevelopment are systematic aspects of late-capitalist urban development. The struggle over the use and production of space is heavily determined by social class and by gender, and is part of the social agenda of a larger restructuring of the economy.

Lesson nine

REQUIRED READING

Neil Smith, "Is Gentrification a Dirty Word?" and "Local Arguments: From 'Consumer Sovereignty' to the Rent Gap" (Chapters 2 and 3, The New Urban Frontier, Rout-ledge, London, 1996).

SUGGESTED READING

Kathryn Nelson, "The Ongoing Need to Assess Gentrification" (Chapter 1, Gentrification and Distressed Cities, The Univ. of Wisconsin Press, 1988).

VIDEO

Video, "La batalla de Euskalduna."

LEARNING GOALS

1. Understand the concept of gentrification.
2. Assess the economic logic that binds together deindustrialization and ruin on the one hand and gentrification and redevelopment on the other.

3. Contextualize Bilbao's transformations in the global logic of urban investment and divestment.
4. Inquire about the ways in which Bilbao's urban development is part of a social agenda for a larger restructuring of the economy.

WRITTEN LESSON FOR SUBMISSION

Please write a two- to three-page essay on one of the topics below.

1. Explain the "rent gap."
2. Is gentrification a rare phenomenon or is it ubiquitous in urban centers?
3. Does consumer sovereignty explain everything about gentrification?
4. Does it make sense to apply the model of gentrification to Bilbao? Why or why not?

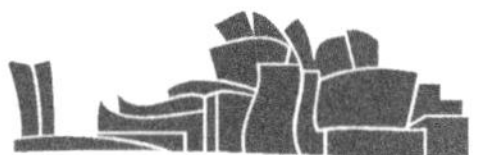

10 · Urban renewal as project and ideology

BY THE END of the 1980s, Basque officials were beginning to accept the unthinkable: the word "decline" referring to Bilbao. Bilbao was the political base of the Basque Nationalist Party and the political force of the region since Franco. An economically and demographically imploding Bilbao sounded several alarms. If the city could be credited with having industrialized the Basque region, it was now time for the country to assist it in its moment of crisis. Bilbao and its greater metropolitan industrial area house half of the two million Basques. For historical, sociological, and financial reasons, it is impossible to reform the Basque economy without first revitalizing its engine, Bilbao.

Thus the entry of the "urban regeneration" discourse and the discovery of the architect as savior. Gehry, Foster, Pelli, Stirling, Wildford, Pei, Soriano, Palacio, Isozaki, and Calatrava are by now household names in Bilbao. The discourse on urban regeneration received public attention when, in 1989, Mayor José María Gorordo organized Bilbao's first international congress, entitled "Forum Bilbao for Urban Regeneration." Throughout the 1980s there had been a huge effort to build a new infrastructure, with highways and bridges at the forefront. But a new beginning was needed, a new image, a new postindustrial economic base, in short, an entire reinvention of the ancient, declining city.

Franco Bianchini was a major influence on Bilbao's cultural policies of city renewal. "Culture" is associated with information, leisure, entertainment, art, travel, and tourism. A common byproduct of advancing industrial economies is an increase in leisure time and activities. So governments invest in cultural services in order to respond to public demands and to create economic diversity and improved social cohesion. Thus, compared with the previous social and political concerns of the 1970s, in which access to culture was paramount, there was a clear shift towards the priority of urban regeneration and economic development. In this atmosphere, cultural policies and urban regeneration strategies became intertwined.

PARTNERSHIPS BETWEEN business and public sectors were a hallmark of the new politics of consensus, and attempts were made to integrate the unemployed, the young, and immigrants into the local community. The emphasis was on the contribution of culture to economy. The actual results of such cultural policies in creating employment and wealth were rather modest, Bianchini admits, on the basis of an analysis of several cities' 1980s cultural policies. Bilbao is illustrative of the effects of changing the city's image and attracting tourism.

There is great variety in the traditions of European nations in determining urban policies. A crucial factor in encouraging the cultural renaissance of provincial cities was the decentralization of power from central to regional governments (Spain provides a strong example). Bilbao's urban renewal in general, and the Guggenheim Museum in particular, cannot be understood outside of the context of Basque local politics. The direct link between Bilbao and New York is a veiled statement of Basque artistic and national sovereignty vis-à-vis Madrid. Cultural strategies, such as Bilbao's museological and urbanistic prominence, were key tools in the hands of local politicians working toward social and political goals. According to the ideology of urban renewal, such cultural policies would benefit everybody equally by promoting new tourist industries, creating

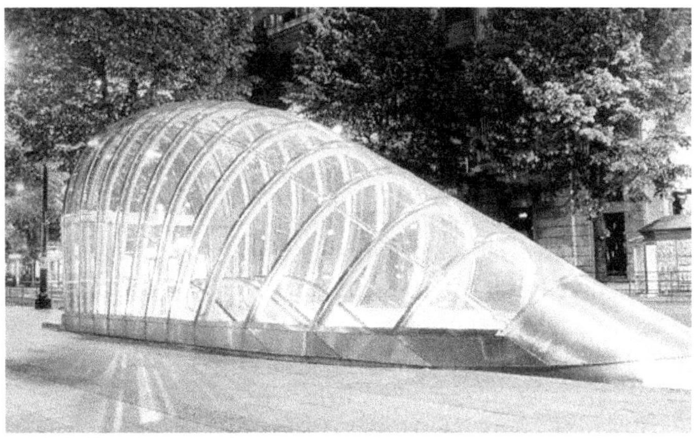

Norman Foster's subway entrance is an emblem of Bilbao's new infrastructure. Money spent on culture and striking public facilities is often an astute investment rather than a subsidy.
Photo by Txetxu Berruezo & Josu Bilbao Fullaondo.

---

employment, and rebuilding the urban community. Thus, political parties could establish a new political base and respond to the decline of their traditional nationalist or working-class constituencies by using urban renewal and flagship architectural projects as means of political communication. Such projects are emblematic of "new" times, and the high-profile cultural policies were symbolic of the break with the provincial policies of the past and provided a vehicle for politicians to take center stage.

The ideology of urban renewal went hand in hand with the 1980s trend towards neoliberalism and neoconservatism. Bilbao illustrates how a decline of traditional social policies can get compensated by new cultural policies, in this case by the promotion of spectacular architecture. These flagship projects were emphasized at the expense of popular creativity and grassroots participation.

ACCESS TO culture or promotion of the arts and publications were categorized as "subsidies," and subsidies for arts and culture were discouraged because of supposed intrinsic problems detrimental to creativity. It was decided that the money once set aside for culture would be better spent on new museums and concert halls that would on their own promote culture and the economy. The discourse of urban regeneration was an easy way to silence critics, because the new spectacular cultural centers were not "subsidy" but a "strategic investment" in the future (an annual subsidy of several million dollars was projected into Bilbao's Guggenheim). Several European cities illustrate the premise that cultural policies can have a huge effect on a city's image. By becoming symbols of a city's rebirth, spectacular buildings are essential to an image strategy, thus, cultural facilities are increasingly important in the competition among similar cities. Julia Gonzalez's article applies the discourse of urban regeneration to Bilbao. Not only did the city have to confront its industrial decline, but Bilbao also faced competition from the other provincial Basque capitals which were becoming administrative and tourist centers.

The alleged antagonism between local and cosmopolitan cultures is one of the ways in which urban renewal discourses try to impose their dominance. "Universal" art and cosmopolitan culture are pitted against local works and, in the case of Bilbao, the tens of millions of dollars cut off from supporting local culture went directly into paying the Guggenheim franchise. Though many writers and artists were critical of such transfers of money, several later came to realize that the success of the Guggenheim also benefited them. The implicit contradictions between the global and regional, between grandiose flagship projects and support for the local arts, can no longer just be viewed through the prism of totalizing urban renewal ideology that only sees benefits and harmonious progress for everyone, but must instead be seen by critics and supporters alike as energizing dilemmas of a new type of culture and identity.

Lesson ten

REQUIRED READING

Franco Bianchini, "Remaking European Cities: The Role of Cultural Policies" (in Cultural Policy and Urban Regeneration: The West European Experience, Bianchini and Parkinson, eds., Manchester Univ. Press, Man-chester, 1993).

Julia González, "Bilbao: Culture, Citizenship and Quality of Life" (in Cultural Policy and Urban Regeneration)

Franco Bianchini, "Culture, Conflict, and Cities: Issues and Prospects for the 1990s" (in Cultural Policy and Urban Regeneration).

LEARNING GOALS

1. Understand the context and meaning of the new discourse of urban renewal.
2. Identify the practical and ideological dimensions of this discourse.

3. Understand the potential effects of cultural policies on economic regeneration.
4. Assess the relationship between urban renewal and image creation.

WRITTEN LESSON FOR SUBMISSION

Please write a two- to three-page essay on one of the topics below.

1. Characterize the "culture" element in the cultural policies of urban renewal.
2. Comment on the practical and ideological roles of the discourse of urban regeneration in Bilbao's resurgence.
3. What are the social and political implications of implementing urban policies?
4. How would you link urban building politics with the politics of national identity?
5. According to Bianchini, what are the three dilemmas of urban cultural policy development?

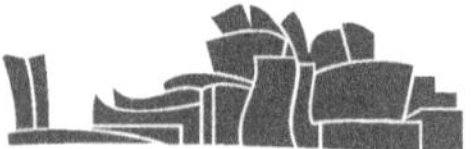

11 · Planning in international context

As a result of the degeneration of the industrial sector, large portions of Bilbao's left bank fell into ruin. These parcels were close to the center and well suited for major redevelopment projects. In the 1990s, an ambitious $1.5 billion urban renewal plan was put in place. The key components of the plan were:

1. Expansion and modernization of the port.
2. New transportation facilities, including a subway (designed by Norman Foster).
3. Expansion of the airport (designed by Santiago Calatrava).
4. Construction of the Zubizuri Bridge (also designed by Calatrava).
5. Creation of an "intermodal" central transport hub for buses and trains (designed by James Stirling, now postponed indefinitely).
6. The Abandoibarra riverfront development, which includes a one million square-foot office and shopping mall complex (designed by Cesar Pelli). See photogrsph on page 83.
7. Construction of theEuskalduna Convention Center and Music Hall (designed by Federico Soriano and Dolores Palacio).
8. Construction of the Bilbao Guggenheim Museum (designed by Frank Gehry).

The Internationalization of the world economy has made it difficult for individual countries and cities to operate in isolation. The European Union has created a single market of 350 million people for its various nation-states; urban planning has clearly been affected. The Single European Act of 1992 removed trade barriers among European nations and increased economic interaction. The conferences on urban regeneration held in Bilbao in the 1980s are an example of the growing interest in exchanging ideas about urban planning theory and practice.

Bilbao's new redevelopment plan revolves around works by star architects coming from the U.S. (Los Angeles), Argentina, Mexico, Great Britain, Japan, and Madrid. The many international forces influencing urban architecture and planning in Bilbao provide a framework to showcase the similarities and differences in their approaches.

Urban planning rests at the interface between market and public interests, and is heavily influenced by political and ideological interests. The theme of "public-private partnership" dominates the arguments concerning appropriate degrees of market intervention. The increased competition among cities to attract tourism and investment has reinforced a trend in national and city governments favoring an entrepreneurial attitude. Bilbao's story illustrates how the urban planning responds simultaneously to local and national political forces as well as global competitive flows. Bilbao also shows that, in similar economic and urban circumstances, other cities could develop the leverage to take risks, be more innovative, and undertake alternative strategies that coiled result in "putting them on the map."

NEWMAN AND Thornley's piece underscores the relevance of the global context in urban planning. The link from world economy and financial systems, to information technologies, to the national deregulation of economic planning, to the new partnerships between business and government urban planning is, indeed, global in nature. Bilbao's story shows how global control of the global economy leads to global control of the museum culture, the art market, and urban planning as a field, anchored by the role of world-renowned architects.

BILBAO ALSO illustrates the declining relevance of nation-states in the renewal of regional cities and the emergence of subnational governments and international institutions in the new global context. Although a Spanish city, Bilbao is also the birthplace of Basque nationalism, which is its dominant political sway in Basque Country. The struggle between Basque and Spanish nationalism are played out in struggles over the direction of Bilbao's ambitious urban renewal, since it will have a powerful effect on the economic and cultural makeup of the entire Basque region. Bilbao's unmediated links with New York's Guggenheim, hailed by international media as the key to the "miraculous" success of the Bilbao Guggenheim project, is a cultural coup for Basque political interests. Art and culture have become major political tools for marginal countries in the global context.

The article by Arantxa Rodríguez details recent trends in urban policymaking in Bilbao. She reviews the crisis in urban planning since the mid-1970s; in her opinion, this crisis was a result of unfulfilled high expectations, inadequate regulatory planning systems for the rapidly changing situation, as well as the extensive reorganization of state policies. The ideology of entrepreneurship and *laissez-faire* capitalism accompanied the withdrawal of the state from social and spatial redistribution. Urban policy gradually assumed more direct support from private capital, and urban planning was substantially reorganized, remaining an important contender in the public arena.

New modes of intervention, planning goals, tools, and institutions emerged, generally devised and financed by central governments. The examples of emblematic large-scale renewals from the U.S. (Boston, Baltimore, and Pittsburgh) and Europe (London, Glasgow, Rotterdam, and Lille) played a significant role in the new urban thinking. The goal was the reconversion of vast derelict sites into mixed-use areas by integrating office space, housing, retail centers, cultural and recreational services, and tourist-oriented infrastructures. This conversion was tied to a radical change in promotional image by using flagship projects, postmodern architecture, theme parks, art festivals, fairs, and so forth, all of which required massive funding. Strong public support and leveraged funding were required to stimulate private sector property and the land market.

THE CREATION OF large, emblematic projects emerged as a viable alternative to the crisis of promulgating a comprehensive plan. These emblematic projects were fragmented and eclectic in their "postmodern" planning, in which aesthetics were paramount. The purpose of these projects is to capture one segment and turn it into the symbol of the new, revitalized metropolis. Waterfront developments epitomize this approach. Peter Hall wrote of one such emblematic project, "Like theater it resembles real life, but it is not urban life as it ever actually was: the model is the Main Street, America exhibit which greets entering visitors at the California Disneyland, sanitized for your protection...."

A swift remake of their urban image is a major goal for many cities in crisis. Such a remake can attract international capital and ease the acquisition of key command functions and high-level producer services. Economic growth is the primary objective, but a remade image plays a crucial role in social representation as a city becomes a living metaphor for the success of its elites. The pitfalls of this mechanism, polarizing effects, an increase in social and spatial inequalities produced by property-led regeneration, contrasts between downtown redevelopment and the unemployment and degradation of the surrounding area, and the risks of two-speed metropolitanization, well illustrated precisely by urban reimaging failures in Pittsburg, Cleveland, Baltimore, and the Docklands in London. In general, Bilbao can serve as a pragmatic example of both the success and potential pitfalls of image based on emblematic buildings.

As shown in the previous chapters, Bilbao's economic and urban restructuring have been massive. Between 1975 and 1991 Bilbao lost 37 percent of its total industrial employment (shipbuilding, steel manufacturing, chemical, electrical equipment, and so on), and the industrial sector went from 45.8 percent of the economy to 31.5 percent. The service sector increased 33 percent during the same period (from 42.8 percent to 58.2 percent). The unemployment rate remained above 20 percent, and towns such as Baracaldo (pop. 130,000) lost 75 percent of its industrial employment and 56 percent of its total employment.

IN SPAIN, THE competence of municipalities that have exclusive jurisdiction over the production of urban plans has been subject to broad guidelines set by the central government. Bilbao remained under the 1964 plan until the ambitious General Urban Plan of Bilbao was approved in 1994. The new plan's two basic objectives were to raise the population's income level and to improve the quality of the urban environment by taking advantage of the areas left behind due to recession. Two abandoned mining sites, a degraded inner city area, an old freight railway line and station to be reconverted

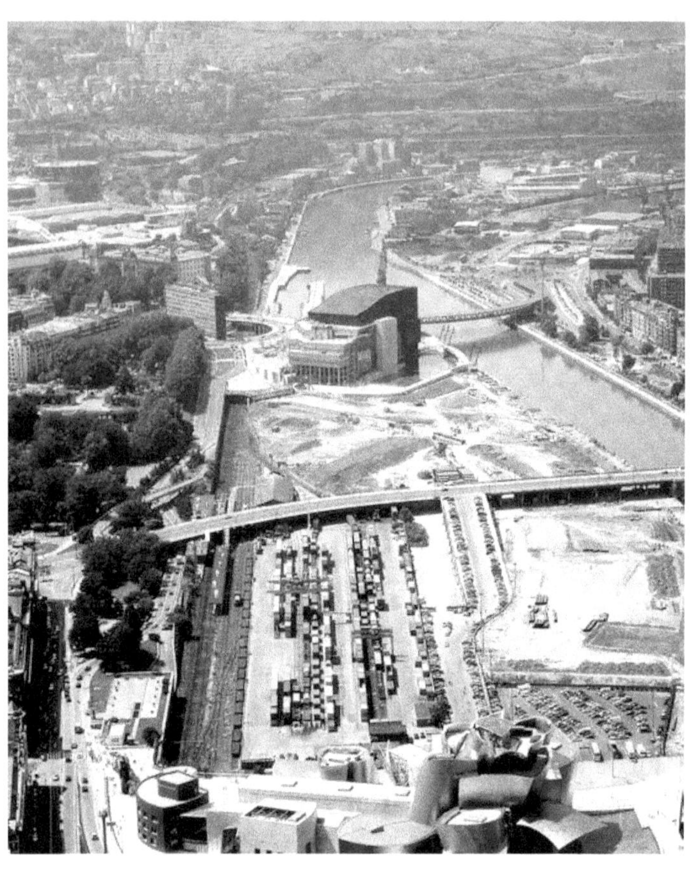

The Abandoibarra riverfront development extends from the Guggenheim museum (seen in part at the bottom of the picture) and the Euskalduna Convention Center and Concert Hall. It includes a million square-foot office and shopping mall complex, designed by Cesar Pelli.
FOAT aerial photography.

into a passenger hub, and 30 hectares of waterfront were added to planned redevelopment area.

According to Rodriguez, the general characteristics of the new plan were:

1. Large emblematic projects
2. A marked downtown bias
3. An attempt to generate public support for property-led redevelopment
4. No socioeconomic content
5. No consideration of social justice issues

At the same time there were continuities with the traditional functional planning that undermined its potential:

1. Exclusive attention to land specifications, transport systems and physical infrastructures
2. Lack of any socioeconomic dimension
3. Unsolved administrative hierarchies between sectoral and spatially sensitive policies
4. Isolation from municipal plans and other proposals for revitalization
5. Lack of implementation mechanisms

The central state holds property claims over a large portion of Bilbao's potential redevelopment sites through firms such as the national railroad company (RENFE), the national institute for industry (INI), and the Port Authority. The need for a coordinated action led to a formal agreement in December 1992 in which the central government and the Basque administration created "Ria 2000," an urban development corporation to promote the regeneration of metropolitan Bilbao, a formally private but in practice quasi-public agency. It has considerable planning powers in setting priorities for intervention and the disposal of land and property for redevelopment. Its mandate is to achieve maximum efficiency through financial self-sufficiency.

Ría 2000 operates much like a private firm, but with public resources of land and money. It manages the risks of development in order to propitiate further private valorization. Among its interventions are the Guggenheim, *Euskalduna*, the convention and concert hall, the urban planning of Abandoibarra, the redevelopment of Amezola (nearly 10 hectares), and the transfer of the railroad from the left bank of the river at the level of Abandoibarra to Amezola. Critical questions about Ria 2000 include the "privatization" of planning and the lack of political accountability. Limited applicability to sites of high commercial potential and overwhelming concern with economic feasibility are also issues. The final question remains whether this form of property-led regeneration will provide sufficient basis for sustained growth.

BILBAO, FOLLOWING a series of debates initiated in 1989, adopted a strategic plan to guide its process of revitalization. Representatives from various economic, administrative, and academic institutions took part in analyzing Bilbao's urban decline and by 1992 it produced the first strategic plan for Bilbao. The plan was comprehensive and metropolitan, but did not succeed. For example, out of 100 organizations and 347 strategies, the Guggenheim was not part of the strategic plan. There was no practical commitment regarding actors, resources, and schedules from the organizations that mattered.

In conclusion, it can be stated that the private sector had the leading role in the urban regeneration while using public funds. Bilbao is an example of property-led regeneration where physical reconstruction of key sites was determined by the requirements of capital restructuring. It is assumed that economic recovery is an automatic outcome of physical renewal, but critical decisions are made on the basis of very partial views on economic restructuring and growth processes. There are risks to a two-speed metropolitanization. The revitalization process is fragmented and there is no public participation.

Lesson eleven

REQUIRED READING

Peter Newman and Andy Thornley, "The International Context" (Chapter 2, Urban Planning in Europe, Routledge, London, 1996).

SUGGESTED READING

Arantxa Rodríguez, "Planning the Revitalization of an Old Industrial City: Urban Policy Innovations in Metropolitan Bilbao" (in Christophe Demazière and Patricia Wilson, eds., Local Economic Development in Europe and the Americas, Mansell, London, 1996).

LEARNING GOALS

1. Learn the basic facts of urban renewal planning in Bilbao.
2. Understand the international European and global contexts in which Bilbao's urban regeneration is taking place.
3. Learn about the transition from earlier urban planning to its present form, in which emblematic projects have the leading role.
4. Critically assess of Bilbao's General Urban Planning's primary characteristics and purposes.

WRITTEN LESSON FOR SUBMISSION

Please write a two- to three-page essay on one of the topics below.

1. Describe the main components of Bilbao's urban renewal planning.
2. Discuss the nature of the private-public partnership in Bilbao's urban regeneration planning.
3. What are the salient traits of the General Urban Plan of Bilbao?
4. Assess critically the need and consequences of large-scale emblematic projects.
5. In which ways is Bilbao's urban renewal dependent on external global forces?

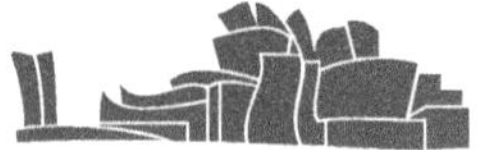

12 · Go, go, Guggenheim

DURING THE LATE 1980s Gorordo, the mayor of Bilbao, in association with the sculptor Oteiza and architect Oiza, proposed a 40,000-square-meter cultural center that would include a library, workshops for artists, a music conservatory, an auditorium, and a museum of contemporary art. Rebellious, paradoxical, authoritarian, and oracular, Oteiza's uncompromising stance in matters of cultural politics brought him into one conflict after another with public officials. Winner of the highest international award at the Biennale of Sao Paulo in 1957, Oteiza was a major influence upon younger generations of artists, but refused to let his work become part of the international art market and declared that he had "concluded" his sculptural phase. All his work lay piled up in the basement of his house, the object of repeated theft attempts.

"The aesthetics of the ugly" was Oteiza's main paradigm when, in 1987, the mayor of Bilbao asked him to develop a contemporary museum and cultural center for the city. However, the project was stalemated by the difficulty of working with the controversial Oteiza. He was always ready to insult officials for their ignorance in artistic matters, and the major was fighting figures in his own party. In November of 1990, having lost the confidence of his party, Gorordo was forced to resign, and his ambitious project was abandoned. But the idea of the cultural center had taken hold of the imagination of the people, and 70,000 citizens signed a document supporting Gorordo's vision.

During this same period, Thomas Krens's financially strapped Guggenheim Museum was knocking at the

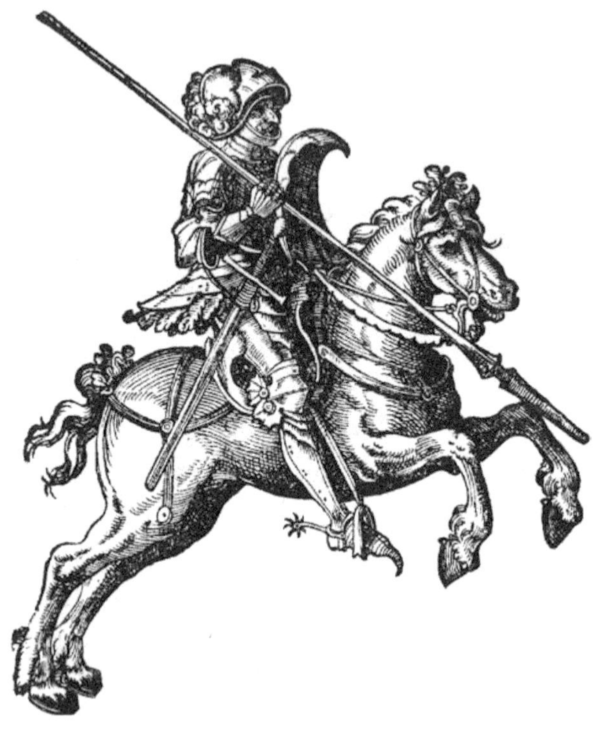

A savior rode to the rescue of a city in ruin and decay. *Woodcut by Jost Amman.*

---

door of various European capitals, including Bilbao, with the proposal of a franchised branch that would boost New York's global reach, while at the same time generating money in the form of fees. A representative of the Guggenheim approached Bilbao's treasury with the offer of a franchised museum in April 1991. Against all odds and in absolute secrecy, the unlikely alliance between Bilbao and the Guggenheim prospered. Why would the leaders of an economically depressed region suddenly put their faith and money into a Guggenheim in Bilbao? Kim Bradley's article describes this "deal of the century."

IT IS FIRST WORTH mentioning the New York Guggenheim's renewal and expansion project under its new director, Thomas Krens, which elicited strong reactions in the press. Armed with a degree in management from Yale, Krens offered the Board of Trustees a choice: to preserve funds and run the museum conservatively, or to change it drastically. Soon the museum had projects going on in New York, Massachusetts, Italy, Austria, and Spain. Krens's goal was to reinvent the museum, using aggressive financial and marketing strategies. He was seen as a visionary by some, and a disaster by others.

In 1989 Krens helped finance the expansion of Frank Lloyd Wright's New York museum by floating $54.9 million in tax-exempt bonds. At that time the Guggenheim had an endowment of $30 million, and critics charged that the collection was in danger. Further controversy surrounded Krens when, in order to acquire the Panza collection of minimalist works, he auctioned three masterpieces from the Guggenheim's collection (a Kandinsky, a Chagall, and a Modigliani) to raise $47.3 million. Critics charged that Krens was treating the masterpieces as "assets."

The other major project by Krens had to do with the franchising of Guggenheim museums worldwide. Critics mocked the idea as a "McGuggenheim" chain and raised issues of the danger posed to the fragile works of art by constant travel. The idea was that the host cities would pay the costs of building the museums and operating the franchises, while New York would be in charge of the artistic direction. After several other European cities declined the offer Krens approached Bilbao officials, and a deal was made.

RICHARDSON'S ARTICLE articulates Krens's agenda. He concludes trenchantly, "The inordinate importance that Krens chooses to attribute to conceptual art and minimalism—the consummate manifestations of the modern movement, he would have us believe—seems much more of a matter of entrepreneurial chauvinism than of any deep artistic conviction. Like most other American businessmen, Krens is out to promote and export his product: art that has been fabricated in the U.S.... Hence, too, his worldwide franchises and the establishment of potentially lucrative links (shades of Disney-world) with hotel and tourist interests. Hence above all, his corporate approach to the museum, which is as conceptual as the merchandise that it has been tailored to market. Krens's incessant talk of 'strategies' recalls the Eighties (so does his taste in art movements), when some financiers devised strategies, not least that of junk bonds, which are in effect a form of conceptual art—to enrich themselves at the expense of virtually everyone else. Indeed, the current Guggenheim schemes can best be understood as a new kind of conceptual art: a combination, perhaps of Boesky and Beuys."

Lesson twelve

REQUIRED READING

John Richardson, "Go, Go, Guggenheim," The New York Review, July 16, 1992.

Kim Bradley, "The Deal of the Century," Art in America, July 1997.

LEARNING GOALS

1. Understand the transformations going on at New York's Guggenheim and its effect on Bilbao.
2. Assess the globalization of the museum.
3. Evaluate auctioning, franchising, and marketing as central strategies to the world or art and museums.
4. Learn about the economic and political context in Bilbao that explains why Basque officials went for Krens's "deal of the century."

WRITTEN LESSON FOR SUBMISSION

Please write a two to three page essay on one of the topics below or choose another relevant topic.

1. Describe the facts of the deal between Krens and Bilbao officials.
2. What are the implications of the construction of the Bilbao Guggenheim Museum for the museum as an institution?
3. Examine the links between urban renewal projects and cultural industries such as museums.
4. Who is dependent on whom—Bilbao on New York, or New York on Bilbao—or are both sides interdependent? What does this new interrelationship reveal?
5. Can we talk about "colonialism" here? If yes, what sort of colonialism is it when the colonizer wants to be colonized? If not, what do you make of the asymmetries in sharing the costs and in the one-sided decision-making process regarding the artistic programs?

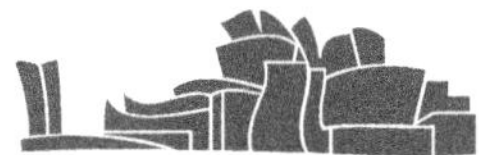

13 · Politics of gambling and seduction

BASQUE POLITICIANS admit that the risks of the Guggenheim Bilbao made the enterprise "like playing in a casino." At the same time, "faith," and what we might call "the politics of belief," became major arguments for the project's promoters. Elsewhere I have described the relationship between Guggenheim director Thomas Krens and Bilbao officials as a complementary process of mutual seduction and risk-taking (*Crónica de una seducción: El Museo Guggenheim Bilbao*, Nerea, Madrid, 1996). Krens defined his main role as follows, "Seduction: that's my business. I am a professional *séducteur*. I don't earn money but I raise it, and I do it by seduction. I make people give me gifts of twenty million dollars. Seduction consists in getting people to want what you want without having to ask for it. It is the transference of desire. I am in a way the greatest prostitute in the world." This is the new atmosphere of late capitalism and its cultural postmodern seductive counterpart.

The phrase that encapsulates the rhetoric of seduction is "I promise." In literature, Don Juan embodies such seductive "perversion of promising," in Shoshana Felman's analysis. "Saying, for him, is in no case tantamount to knowing, but rather to *doing*: *acting* on the interlocutor, modifying the situation and the interplay of forces within it. Language, for Don Juan, is performative and not informative; it is a field of enjoyment, not of knowledge." (*The Literary Speech Act*, Cornell, University Press, 1983, 27). A promise is nothing but a speech act and, even if the seducer has no intention of keeping his promises, still, he does not lie, for all he is doing is playing on the self-referential property of language. Seduction consists in the referential illusion by which a merely linguistic act becomes the basis for an extralinguistic act of commitment.

Essentially, Krens was offering Bilbao promises. In the discourse of promising (marriage, love, happiness), Don Juan plays with the referential illusion of a verbal act which escapes the hold of truth. Again, the seducer is not, strictly speaking, lying, but simply playing with the self-referential illusion of words. This skillful exploitation of "the specular structure" of language by which he makes others *believe* in his promises without himself having to, is Don Juan's scandal. To paraphrase Krens, it is a matter of making others desire that which you want them to, of making of them believers in a course of action that you, yourself, have apparently not demanded and for which you, therefore, cannot be held responsible. In short, the skilled *séducteur* creates the demand, surreptitiously, for the product that he will then supply.

During his first visit to Bilbao, Krens, playing the vulnerable seducer, asked his hosts why they were they interested in the Guggenheim. He received the perfect answer: "The country needs a challenge, and this is going to be it." Jean Baudrillard argues, "Challenge and seduction are quite similar. And yet there is a difference. In a challenge one draws the other into one's area of strength.... Whereas in a strategy of seduction one draws the other into one's area of weakness, which is also his or her area of weakness ... isn't the panther's scent itself a weakness, an abyss which the other animals approach giddily?" (*Seduction*, St. Martin's Press, 1979, 83).

WHAT COULD KRENS promise Bilbao? Access to the entire world of art, museums, Wall Street contacts, plus all the glamour of New York. He toured European capitals with Bilbao representatives and introduced

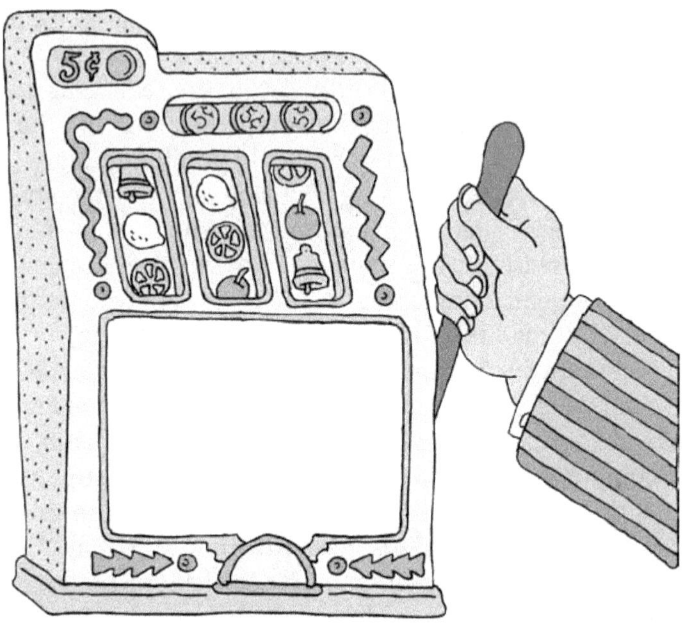

Basque politicians gambled on a dazzling vision, and called it a challenge. Comments from the public were not invited.
Illustration: Seymour Chwast

---

them to diplomats, architects, and museum directors—all part of a dazzling strategy. It would all be theirs if only they dared to believe in him and make a firm written commitment to the terms he needed to impose. It was not that the Bilbao officials were unaware of the project's large risks; but this was not a time for timidity, but rather one for seduction, gambling, and faith. This was postmodern Bilbao.

Wall Street's stock market is a casino for capitalists. American critics repeatedly compared Krens's financial tactics with the junk bond maneuvers of the 1980s. More to the point, it is not surprising that Basque President José Antonio Ardanza (1985–1998) appeared on Wall Street to sign the Guggenheim deal, delivering a check for the $20 million down payment. In Bilbao, the presentation of the Guggenheim design by Gehry also took place at the stock exchange, underscoring the direct connections among the worlds of art, architecture, international capital, and the auction houses. The formally dressed people in attendance had had to cross a picket line of unemployed workers shouting, "thieves!" "scoundrels!" and "fewer museums and more jobs!" It was then and there that Gehry first spoke of Bilbao's "magic," of its being his "idea of heaven," and of the project being "a perfect dream."

SUCH UNEASY encounters between the designs of the elite and the shouts of the unemployed are also a part of "tough Bilbao" (see chapter nineteen). This was also the period in which "catharsis" became the central concept with which public officials addressed the needs of Basque art and culture. It was a simple matter of mathematics; the Guggenheim had to be paid for. Twenty million dollars was needed to pay for the franchise, $100 million for the building, $20 million for the urbanization of the surroundings, $50 million for the art, plus an indeterminate annual subsidy of several million. Eighty percent of all public funding for museums began to go to the Guggenheim. The funds were taken directly from the Basque Government's Ministry of Culture, which was forced to slash its support for other traditionally subsidized activities. This led to the catharsis that libraries, subsidized publications, research, cinema, theater, literature, and popular arts, not to mention other museums, had to undergo, reducing their budgets by an average of 20 to 30 percent. The catharsis was accompanied by a conceptual shift in public discourse which justified the change of policy as slashing "subsidies" (with all the negative connotations of sterilizing creativity) in favor of "strategic investment" in the future.

THE INVESTMENT has started to pay off in tourism and a reinvigorated service sector in Bilbao's economy. Close to one 100,000 people visit the Guggenheim monthly, half of them from outside the Basque Country. Krens's seduction has triumphed, over the objections of his critics; yet that triumph has brought about a paradoxical triumph as well: the debris of history represented by Basque industrial and anthropological ruins, the outdated cultural perspectives of local artisans and entrepreneurs, the evaporated aura of tradition and vanishing local crafts have, paradoxically, been elevated by their thematization as objects of contemplation in the Guggenheim, and reinvigorated by being incorporated in Bilbao's "tough city" image.

Thus Bilbao is once again searching out adventure and golden opportunities amid suspiciously "non-Basque" cultural content from the outside world. Once again Bilbainos are blazing a Basque trail into the new global world. Basques are once again "Vizcainos," as in the time of Don Quixote. At a cost of $100 per Basque, or $700 per Bilbaino, only Bilbao could grant Frank Gehry the opportunity to build a museum that not even the Disney Corporation and his home city Los Angeles felt they could afford during the 1990s.

The Nervíon River has been criss-crossed by the new bridges of *Rontegi*, *Euskalduna*, and *Zubizuri*, and

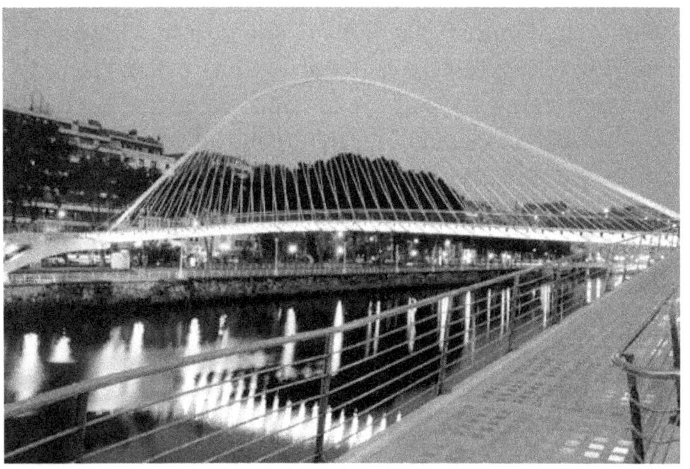

The Zubizuri bridge, designed by Santiago Calatrava. The Nervión River had been bridged long before the villa was founded in 1300. Recent structures cross it at several points.
Photo by José Alberto Gandía

---

others are in the planning stage. But the real bridge that matters now is the one linking Bilbao with New York. It doesn't seem to be enough to promote industrial, infrastructural, or transformative economies that bring in real dollars. Now the true measure of success appears to be the bridging of transatlantic distances by facilitating traffic in modern art, museum franchises, journalistic images, and funds for cultural patrimony. The only bridge that matters now for Bilbao is to become the fundamental museological *point de repère* of the so-called "Atlantic Arc" stretching from Santiago de Compostela to Bordeaux. Bilbao, too, has to welcome the newly imagined, global postmodern space of late capitalism.

In short, there is one crucial difference between the first wave of industrialization a century and a half ago and this postindustrial transformation. It is the difference between a mine and a casino. The mining industry too had an "El Dorado" mentality of fortune seeking and adventure. But success depended mostly on the quantifiable variables of work, transport, management, productivity, and finance. This capitalist logic, one assumes, is still necessary, but other intangibles seem to be as important, or more so, in the new postindustrial world. Suddenly, concepts such as "image," "flagship," "perception," "challenge," "chance," and "the media" become crucial. These are notions that at first sight might appear to be arbitrary, but analysis reveals them to be essential elements of the new culture of postmodernism. Bilbao's sudden "miracle" is the best illustration of it to date.

THE "CASINO" ANALOGY is not mere metaphor. It is evident that, in the ongoing revitalization of Bilbao, such intangibles as gamblers' faith, emblematic symbolism, architecturally imprinted sacredness, the promising logic of seduction, and potlatch-like ritual components are central. It is a new sort of millennialism, as befits this period of "endings." The discourse itself plays a crucial role in creating the new reality.

Consider the element of gambling in the world of art and museums. Analysts have characterized the international art community as a product of the auction market, which was clearly evidenced by Krens' behavior. Krens achieved notoriety in the New York art world by auctioning masterpieces from the museum's permanent collection to buy minimalist works. Members of the committee of experts created by the Basque Cultural

---

Ministry were convinced that Krens wanted to use Bilbao's 5 billion pesetas granted for art purchases to bid at Sotheby's.

Krens made it clear that Bilbao's real contribution was not money, but rather "the patent" upon a new museological design. Twenty million dollars is not a huge sum in the rarefied atmosphere of museum finances, but it represents a quantum leap in conceptual and symbolic terms—the absolute historic novelty of a franchised museum. It signals the era in which a New York director is also the director of a museum branch across an ocean, 4,000 miles away.

GLOBAL MUSEUM franchises can work, and the Bilbao Guggenheim proves it. Architectural designs, museum programs, art exhibits, art purchases, and the management of museums can be marketed from Wall Street across the world, just like McDonald's hamburgers. There is the costs of expensive exhibits to share; but, more importantly, new international franchising makes the Guggenheim the most attractive museum for global capital. This factor that has been labeled decisive by such tycoons as Ronald O. Perelman, chairman of Revlon and president of the Guggenheim Board at the time of the deal, and Peter B. Lewis, who pledged $50 million to Krens with the comment, "I think the Guggenheim is a fascinating and important dream. It's now a worldwide institution, and institutions of this kind should be fostered." The "global" museum patent is paying off for Krens, and it is what makes the Guggenheim particularly attractive for a global capital market that includes the arts and now museums. And Bilbao was the city that went for it.

This image-oriented new ideology of urban regeneration needs the international star-architect aura as much as fish need water. In Bilbao, the subway, the Abandoibarra, the transport hub, the superport, and industrial park all bear the signatures of stars but cannot be financed by local capital alone. Ardanza's second visit to Wall Street was to seek underwriters for Basque public debt. The great news is, as we will see in future chapters, that the gamble is, so far, paying off.

Lesson thirteen

Required Reading

Robin Cembalest, "The Guggenheim's High-Stakes Gamble," ARTnews, May 1992.

Andrew Decker, "What Price Guggenheim?" Village Voice, June 23, 1992.

Susanna Andrews, "Self-Confidence Man," New York Magazine, May 9, 1994.

SUGGESTED READING

Selma R. Holo, "Negating the Center in Bilbao" in S. R. Holo, Beyond the Prado: Museums and Identity in Democratic Spain, Smithsonian Institution, Washington, 1999.

LEARNING GOALS

1. Identify the museological and political contexts of the financial transactions that took place between Bilbao and the Guggenheim
2. Bilbao and the mentality of risk-taking
3. The search for a new definition of the museum
4. Basque politics of building

WRITTEN LESSON FOR SUBMISSION

Please write a two- to three-page essay on one of the topics below.

---

1. In what way are the Basques playing in the casino of globalism?
2. Describe the economic and artistic roles New York and Bilbao play in the high-stakes museum franchise gamble.
3. Discuss the politics of belief, risk-taking, and seduction.
4. Comment on Krens's definition of the museum as "providing space to seduction by incongruity."

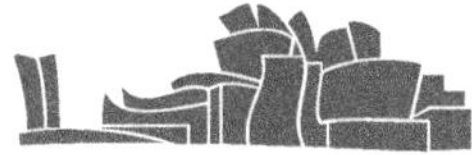

14 · Whose art is it?

WALTER BENJAMIN'S essay argues that the most distinctive aspect of modern art is the capacity for much of it to be mechanically reproduced. Art is, in principle, always reproducible, but something entirely new happens to the audience of art because of mechanical reproduction. The traditional crafts of engraving, etching, stamping and founding give way in the nineteenth century to lithography and then to photography and the reproduction of sound. What reproductions lack is the presence of the original author's time and space, the work's unique existence and authenticity. In the classical crafts, the original has authority vis-a-vis its copy. Such a relationship of original to copy is lost in the technical reproduction of the modern work of art (for example, the photograph can capture images which elude natural vision, and a copy can put an original in situations that are out of reach for the original itself).

What withers in the age of mechanical reproduction? The aura of the work of art. Mechanical reproduction liquidates the traditional value of the cultural heritage. For Benjamin, looking at tradition and the uniqueness of a work of art is what was previously the basis of the authentic, ritual appreciation of a work of art. This idea later turned into the theology of *l'art pour l'art*. With mechanical reproduction art becomes emancipated from ritual. If, in prehistoric times, the art value was, put simply, an instance of magic, today its value is purely exhibitionistic. The artistic function is recognized as incidental (as in photography and film). Similarly the movie camera replaces the theater audience. On stage the actor has to identify with the character of his / her role, but there is as little "acting" as possible in films or

TV, much of it is done "mechanically," in large part because there is no unity of time in film production: that is, scenes are shot and edited together. Benjamin compares the strangeness of the actors in front of the camera with the way we feel before our own image in the mirror. It is a reflected image of the actor that is separable and transportable to the public.

Barthes took these ideas further and proclaimed "the death of the author." "Writing," he claimed, "is the destruction of every voice, of every point of origin. Writing is that neutral, composite, oblique space where our subject slips away, the negative where all identity is lost." Barthes sees literature as tyrannically centered in the author, though the language, not the author, is the primary speaker. Mallarmé's poetics consisted in suppressing the author in the interest of writing; having recourse to the interiority of the writer was superstition. Surrealism's experiences in automatic and communal writing went one step farther in desacralizing the role of the author. The removal of the author utterly transforms the modern text, and writing becomes no longer a representation but rather a performative act in which the main content of the enunciation is the act of being uttered. The book itself becomes only a tissue of signs, a multidimensional space in which a variety of writings blend and clash.

THIS INTELLECTUAL climate helps explain some debates in the art world, such as the one between Judd and Panza, examined by Patricia Failing. Panza bought paper sketches of possible works of art from Judd, which he later developed in his workshop without the consent of Judd. These were exhibited in ways that were inappropriate to the artist. Judd vigorously denied that some of the "Judds" in Panza's exhibit were his. In fact, of the twenty-seven works in his name, Judd only

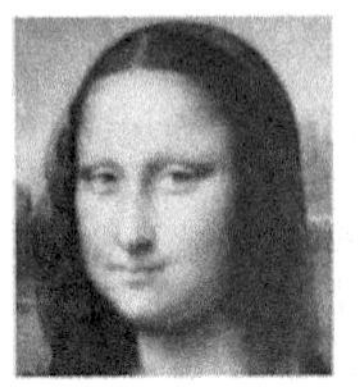
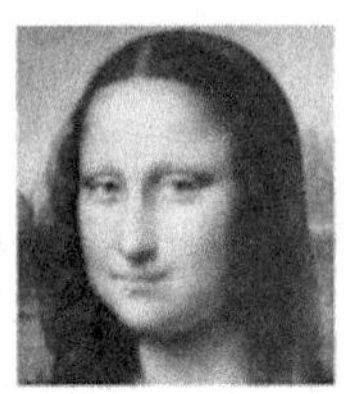
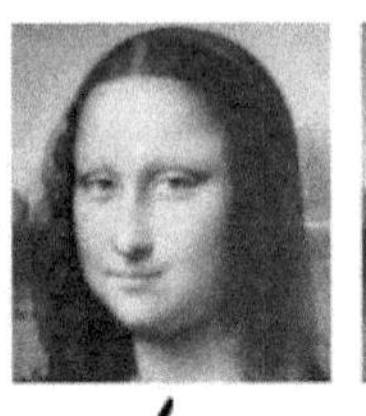
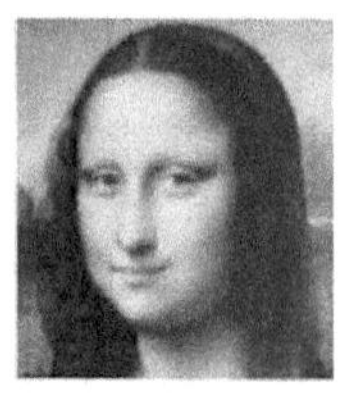

✓

What is a "genuine reproduction?" All five are much the same. The original painting represents the Mona Lisa. The copies can only represent the painting.
Illustration based on the original in the Louvre Museum.

---

recognized thirteen as his own. Obviously, this polemic between the artist and the collector has direct bearings on notions such as intellectual property and work ownership and says nothing of ideas such as "originality," "authenticity," or "authorship." Despite the very public protests by Judd, Panza sold the collection to the Guggenheim for its exhibition at Krens's Mass MOCA projected museum. When that project failed, the collection was headed for Bilbao.

Another illustration of the difficulties in determining authenticity of an author / artist involves Krens's purchase of Beuyses, that later were deemed to be false, for Bilbao.

Panza did not have the copyright of Judd's work, but had purchased from the artist a license to create some works under certain circumstances. This practice raises legal and ethical issues because Panza was buying only "the idea," not the artistic objects themselves. But the artists disagree. Robert Morris, another artist collected by Panza, argued that his "sculptures were realized as copies, not original works, each new installation adding new work, polemically against the precious objects." Are such works originals (that a collector can keep and sell as a unique work of art) or are they copies? Another Panza-collected artist, Carl Andre charged that Panza had made a "gross falsification" of his work because "my works are unique material conditions." Judd added, "To me, a single piece is a single piece, just like in the old days." "I am not a conceptual artist," he concluded. Likewise, Panza knowingly recreated Dan Flavin's destroyed "green crossing greens" (which Flavin had dedicated to Piet Mondrian, "who lacked green"). Flavin destroyed this work in 1966 (in Eindhoven) and Panza recreated it without any authorization from the artist.

IT IS STILL UNCLEAR what the Guggenheim bought from Panza. There is no precedent for these kinds of acquisitions. These new relationships among artists, collectors, and museums are indicative of fundamental changes in the nature of the work of art. The mechanical reproduction of art and the questioning of artistic authorship have created anomalies yet to be resolved. The latest exhibits of Krens's Guggenheim—a collection of motorcycles and a collection of Armani suits—raise similar issues of whose art is it.

Lesson fourteen

REQUIRED READING

Patricia Failing, "Judd and Panza Square Off," ARTnews, Nov. 1990.

Andew Decker, "Can the Guggenheim Pay the Price?" ARTnews, Jan. 1994.

SUGGESTED READING

Joseph Beuys, Jannis Kounellis, Anselm Kiefer, Enzo Cucchi, "The Cultural-Historical Tragedy of the European Continent" (in Charles Harrison and Paul Wood, Art in Theory: 1900–1990. Blackwell, Oxford, 1992, 1032–36).

Roland Barthes, "The Death of the Author" (In R. Barthes, Image, Music, Text, Hill and Wang, New York, 1977).

Walter Benjamin, "The Work of Art in the Age of Mechanical Reproduction" (in Illuminations, Shocken, 1968).

LEARNING GOALS

1. Examine the transformation undergone by art under the influence of modern technologies.
2. Question ideas of authenticity and authorship in contemporary culture in the context of "mechanical reproduction."
3. Consider the debates between artists and collectors about the ownership of their work.
4. Understand the direct bearing of such issues on the Guggenheim Bilbao.

WRITTEN LESSON FOR SUBMISSION

Please write a two- to three-page essay on one of the topics below.

1. What are the substantive differences between the collector and the artist in the Panza / Judd debate?
2. How would you judge the mediation of the collector and the museum in the relationship between the artist and the public?
3. Should the Bilbao Guggenheim Museum care about auctioning, faking, or making copies without authorization of the artist? Why or why not?
4. Discuss what you see as the positive and negative sides of the work of art losing its "aura."

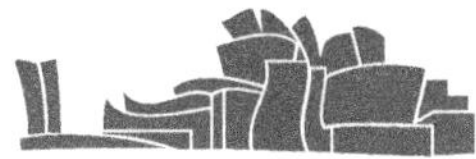

15 · McDonald's global museum model?

KRENS'S IDEA OF A galaxy of satellite museums, run from New York and paid by the host cities soon engendered an analogy to the McDonald's chain. The prospective franchised museums were widely derided as "McGuggenheims," and there is more than casual disparagement to the analogy. Museums are not immune to the globalizing forces in the culture and economy of the last two decades. Although criticized for some of his ideas, Krens is the one museum director who has dared to apply to the museum strategies and perspectives are common in other fields. The McDonaldization of society is after all, as argued by Ritzer, a pervasive phenomenon that increasingly affects substantial domains of our public institutions.

"McDonaldization" refers to "the process by which the principles of the fast-food restaurant are coming to dominate more and more sectors of American society as well as the rest of the world." (McDonald's began franchising in 1955 and by 1991 had opened 12,000 outlets in the U.S. alone.) A wide array of other fast-food businesses adopted the same model (Taco Bell, Pizza Hut, Sbarro's, Popeye's), as well as more "upscale" restaurants such as Sizzler, Fudrucker, and Red Lobster. The leading 100 restaurant chains operate more than 110,000 outlets in the U.S. (one for every 2,250 Americans), a phenomenon that now has a global reach. By 1991 McDonald's was annually opening more restaurants abroad (427) than in the U.S. (188). McDonald's, as a symbol, has been appropriated as a nickname by many other businesses, such as McDentists, McDoctors, McChild Care Centers, McStables, McPaper, etc. It has come to occupy a central place in the popular culture of movies and television shows; it is, in short, a universally recognized symbol, for better or for worse, of Americanism. McDonaldization shows up in shopping malls, hospitals, university campuses, highway driving, and airports. For many, very private aspects of our lives, including religion and sex, have become McDonaldized.

Ritzer finds four basic dimensions to the pervasiveness of McDonaldization:

1. Efficiency. Essential for a fast-paced society, whether for getting rid of hunger, lubricating cars, or losing weight.
2. Service. Easily quantified and calculated, even if the calculation might be illusory.
3. Predictability. Offering a world with no surprises.
4. Control. In particular, by substituting technology for human labor, and by routinizing the remaining human labor. Workers in fast-food restaurants can do very limited things, and only precisely the way they are trained to.

MAX WEBER STUDIED a precursor to McDonaldization, which he called the "iron cage" of modern bureaucratization and rationalization. Henry Ford's assembly line of robot-like workers, the mass-produced suburban houses of Levittown, the shopping mall, and the original McDonald's are all examples. The McDonald brothers opened their first restaurant in Pasadena, California, in 1937, relying on the quantifiable variables of speed, volume, and low price. They utilized assembly-line procedures for cooking and serving food and developed rules dictating what workers should and should not do and say. Ray Kroc made McDonald's the empire that it is today by franchising, a business model pioneered by the Singer Sewing Machine company after the Civil War and soon utilized by automobile

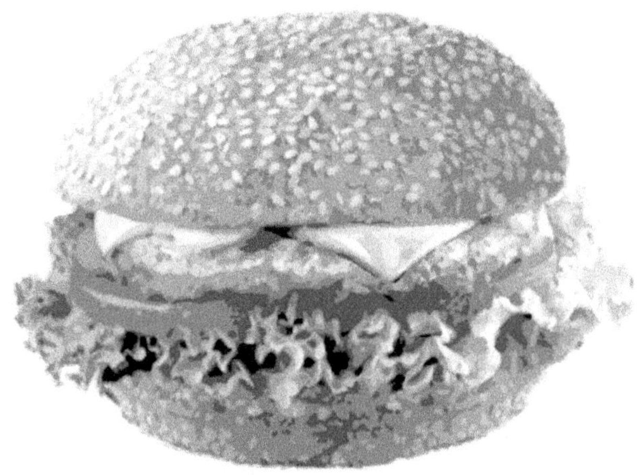

Hearing about the McDonald's hamburger stand in California, Ray Kroc packed up his car and headed West. It was 1954. He was 52 years old.

---

manufacturers and soft-drink companies. All Kroc needed was the ambition to turn McDonald's, through franchising, into a national business. Thus, Richter stresses, McDonaldization does not represent something new, but rather the culmination of a trend already in existence.

Thomas Krens was taken by many as a would-be Ray Kroc of franchised museums. All he had to do was expand upon a recent development: borrowing entire art collections from other museums for a fee. This idea was thought up by the financially troubled Boston Museum of Art, which lent art for a fee to the Japanese city of Nagoya. Soon other museums had similar arrangements to lend one another collections. But Krens was the first one to apply the franchise model to a museum by imposing the original name and demanding a license fee of $20 million. The McDonaldized elements—efficiency, calculability, predictability, and above all, control—are present and in good order in Krens's reinvention of the museum as part of a global galaxy of museums. There are positive aspects to the model, attested to by success of the Bilbao Guggenheim; however, there are also grounds for concern and criticism. It is worth mentioning some of the general criticisms of the McDonaldization model.

IN WEBERIAN TRADITION, Ritzer claims that McDonaldization is part of "the irrationality of rationality." He points out the social costs of McDonaldization, resulting in inefficiency, unpredictability, incalculability and loss of control. Ritzer cites a good summation by Richard Cohen, who calls it the "ATM rule of life": "I was told—nay promised—that I could avoid lines at the bank and make deposits or withdrawals any time of the day. Now, there are lines at the ATMs, the bank seems to take a percentage of whatever I withdraw or deposit, and, of course, I'm doing what tellers (remember them?) used to do. Probably, with the new phone, I'll have to climb telephone poles in the suburbs during ice storms." In brief, the new arrangements are often more expensive, force consumers to do unpaid work, and are inefficient. So, for whom is the

McDonaldized world efficient? For the bank, the gas station, the supermarket, the telephone company, and, of course, for McDonald's. The fast-food principles imposed on the hordes of teenagers working at minimum wage are highly efficient for those at the top, not for workers and the consumers. Another application is the mass production of fun, efficiently doled out like a an anesthetic at McDonaldized entertainment parks such as Disneyland.

IN THE RELATIONSHIP between the Bilbao and New York Guggenheim, Bilbao had to pay a franchise fee for the name and expertise for starters, and then vast amounts for construction, the purchase of new works of art, the arrangements of exhibits, and operating and insurance costs. However, all the artistic decisions (what to buy, whom to exhibit, and how to advertise) are made in New York. The franchised efficiency is premised on Bilbao footing the bill for capital and operating costs without intruding on the artistic and intellectual judgments that guide its museum. In case anyone had any complaints, Krens made himself the artistic director of Bilbao's Guggenheim as well.

A crucial aspect of the deal between New York and Bilbao was the ability of Bilbao Guggenheim to systematically borrow parts of the New York's modernist collections for exhibits. The initial expectation of seeing all the emblematic works by the great modernist masters in Bilbao has yet to come to fruition. What really drives the operations of the museum, garnering media attention and attracting tourists, are the temporary exhibits. The fact that these changing exhibits, rather than a permanent collection, have become the centerpiece of the museum's day to day functioning is one more dimension of the globalized world of fast information and large-scale travel. It denotes a crucial transformation in the classic function of museums as temples, where visitors could come to continually put themselves in contact with revered classical works.

Lesson fifteen

REQUIRED READING

George Ritzer, "McDonaldization and Its Precursors," and "The Iron Cage of McDonaldization?" (Chapters 2 and 8, The McDonaldization of Society, Pine Forge Press, Thousand Oaks, 1993).

Tom Rosenthal, "Kentucky Fried Guggenheim," Art Review, June 1998.

SUGGESTED READING

Hilton Kramer, "Dispersing a Museum Collection," The New Criterion, September 1992.

LEARNING GOALS

1. Understand the impact of the historical globalizing forces on the institution of the museum.
2. Examine the McDonald's model and its potential application to museums.
3. Consider the franchise aspect of the Bilbao Guggenheim.
4. Garner a comprehensive and critical understanding of such historical transformations in the institution of the museum.

WRITTEN LESSON FOR SUBMISSION

Please write a two- to three-page essay on one of the topics below.

1. Examine the influence of globalization on the museum world.

2. Describe the McDonaldization model.
3. How do you assess the effect of the application of the franchise model to the museum? In which ways is it problematic? What historical trends are imposing this direction?
4. Discuss the interplay between permanent collections and temporary exhibits in the museum. How is that relationship changing, and what does this change reveal?

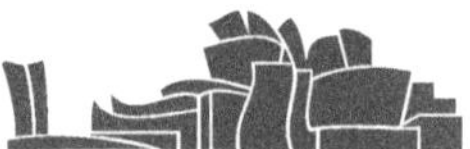

16 · "Miracle in Bilbao"

THE OPENING OF Bilbao's Guggenheim made stunning international news, showcasing Bilbao's process of urban and economic renewal. The *New York Times* led the chorus of ecstatic reviews in its Sunday magazine, labeling the spectacular building "Miracle in Bilbao." The cover displayed a photograph of the Guggenheim Bilbao museum, astride the city's Nervión River, bathed in glittering yellows, whites, and reds. Gehry's white titanium whale at sunset, drenched in the torrid, golden, crackling flames of sodium lamps, loomed over the river like a miraculous specter of the shut-down *Altos Hornos*.

The fabled blast furnaces of the steel-making plant that nourished thousands of families for a century now stand idle, just one of the many ruins that stand as haunting, pitiful reminders of the lost grandeur of Bilbao (chapter eight). Yet, the radiance of Gehry's spectacle is transforming the left bank's wasteland. The caption of the photograph for the cover of the *New York Times Magazine* reads: "The word is out that miracles still occur, and that a major one is happening here. ... 'Have you seen Bilbao?' In architectural circles, the question has acquired the status of a shibboleth. Have you seen the light? Have you seen the future?"

The one man most responsible for this miracle was its architect, Frank Gehry. Thomas Krens brought Gehry to Bilbao after making "the deal of the century" with the Basque government. For Muschamp, the Bilbao Guggenheim was "a Lourdes for a crippled culture," and the first words were an admonition to his American readers: "If you want to look into the heart of American art today, you are going to need a passport" and find your way to Bilbao. It seemed that the last thing in Muschamp's mind during his visit to Bilbao was to find out anything about the history of the now-ruined blast furnaces or about the culture of the city that undertook such a high-stakes gamble. In keeping with the style of globalization, for the critic the Bilbao Guggenheim masterpiece has practically nothing to do with local cultural politics and everything to do with the messianism of a heroic architect.

Gehry himself had a different take on the discourse of "the miracle." In his interviews he insisted that "the miracle is that it has been built at all." What was most significant for Gehry was that Bilbao, and not his home city of Los Angeles, would have dared to risk building such an unorthodox museum. During the 1990s Gehry battled unsuccessfully with various agencies over the construction of the Disney Concert Hall in downtown Los Angeles, an earlier design similar to Bilbao's. An understanding of the historical and political circumstances of the host city, such as we have attempted in the first part of this course, is essential to any analysis of the miracle.

WHAT IS HAPPENING in Bilbao can be considered the cutting edge of the future of the Basque community as an urban, economic, political, and cultural entity. Understanding the transformation of Bilbao poses major intellectual challenges, both in relation to the external images Basques project, as well as in relation to what kind of society and economy they want for themselves. Bilbao is the elementary school where Basques are learning about themselves and their role in the world.

For centuries, Basques were known in Spain as "Vizcainos." In Shakespeare's time, "Bilbo" was the

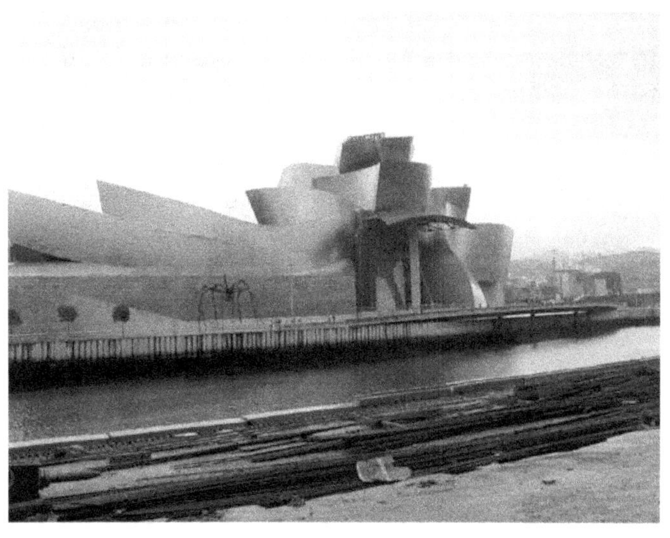

Bilbao now has its landmark with New York glamor and the global culture of spectacle.
Photo: Ibon Aranberri.

---

name of a sword made of Vizcaya's famed steel. For a world fixated on the discourse of terrorism, anything "Basque" harbors an association with arms and violence. But thanks to the Guggenheim Museum, Bilbao now makes different news. The significance cannot be overestimated. In our postmodern globalized world, economic regeneration is as much about image as it is about investment and production. The three elements go hand in hand, creating a dynamic in which symbolic elements play a crucial role.

Were the Basques visionaries? Theorists may wonder which Basque Country and which Basque diaspora the future will yield. How will today's visualizations influence future city formations? For Basques, nothing is as visible as Bilbao's stunning transformation in image and psychology as the result of the Guggenheim Effect. Basques might become known as "Bilbainos," providing the world with "Bilbainadas" (exorbitant projects that appear to be so out of sync with the resources at hand that they become jokes that transform into spectacular successes). Basques are fortunate to have the original patent.

IT IS IMPOSSIBLE to discuss notions such as "Basque identity" or "Basque history" without considering Bilbao. It is the womb of Basque industry and finance, and the prime force in shaping Basque society, politics, and culture. The vast scale of economic production and urban growth and the highly successful symbiosis of international capital and local elite are unique Bilbao phenomena. Because of the massive influx of migrant workers from the Basque and Spanish regions, urban and rural Basque society meet and mingle in Bilbao. It is also where Euskadi articulates with Spain, Europe, and the world. Bilbao is the birthplace of the two main ideological systems of the Basque Country: the Basque Nationalist Party and the Spanish Socialist Party. And yet, if we take into account the most "typical" representations of Basque culture as studied by linguistics and anthropology, Bilbao is the least "Basque" part of Basque Country. For example, only 8 percent of Bilbainos speak Euskera, compared with 35 to 40 percent of the inhabitants of San Sebastián.

A contradiction lies at the center of the problems and capacities of a local identity in the globalized world.

IN BILBAO, TO put the paradox in dialectical terms, the forces of globalization are nursing their antithesis. By attracting and absorbing non-Basque elements Balbao has, at the same time, redefined, reinvigorated, and reasserted an antagonistically Basque historical legacy. This perspective is crucial to an understanding of what is happening in postindustrial Bilbao. The city has formally opted to navigate in the foreign waters of New York glamour and the global culture of spectacle rather than address the local realities of cultural continuity and social needs.

Bilbao's officials feel they understand what history requires of their city and their society if they are not to remain marginalized in the face of the triumphs and failures of modernity. Faced with a new sense of challenge and renewal, Bilbao has a crucial role to play.

Lesson sixteen

REQUIRED READING

Herbert Muschamp, "The Miracle in Bilbao." New York Times Magazine, Sept. 7, 1997, 56 59, 72, 82.

"A 'Miracle' of the 'Times'." The New Criterion, Oct. 17, 1997.

VIDEO

ABC Nightline video, Oct. 10, 1997.

LEARNING GOALS

1. Evaluate the impact of the Guggenheim on Bilbao's international image.

2. Trace the transition from the politics of belief to the discourse of "the miracle."
3. Situate the new museum within Bilbao's historical tradition of economic and urban reinvention.
4. Understand the massive interaction of local and global forces in the construction of one concrete building.

WRITTEN LESSON FOR SUBMISSION

Please write a two- to three-page essay on one of the topics below.

1. Where is the miracle? Comment on the primacy of the architectural dimension of the museum project as a whole.
2. Describe the changes that have made Bilbao's image transformation so spectacular.
3. Examine the role of the media in defining and promoting the hegemony of the new architecture and the new global museum.
4. Provide the contrasting global and local perspectives of the significance of the changes brought about by the founding of the Bilbao Guggenheim.

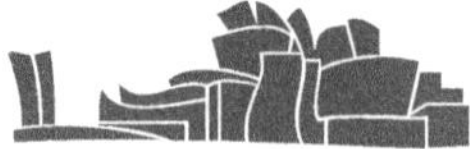

17 · Gehry's Apotheosis

A STORYTELLER MIGHT begin Bilbao's tale like this: Once upon the time there was a city full of ruins that wanted to be Las Vegas. One day it suddenly realized that decay and obsolescence and pollution abounded on its shores and rivers and in its once-beautiful valleys. That night it dreamt of turning entirely to gold and becoming a shining bright star in the glamorous firmament of art, museums, make-believe, and tourism. The next morning was a new day. When light returned at dawn it was time to awake as usual, but the city's people decided not to wake up and instead to continue dreaming. Life had to go on, however, so bakeries and coffee shops and newspaper stands opened. The signs of somnambulism were hard to detect. While Bilbao was enjoying its intoxicated dream state, someone at the other end of the world was in a sleepless frenzy. He was destined to save the city by making its dreams come true. The providential shaman, who would make voyages to the land of the unknown, was an architect. This guardian angel of Bilbao's dream worked in Santa Monica ....

"Heroic" was the one word that Krens used to define the Guggenheim-Bilbao project. Gehry was sent to Bilbao for the heroic call, the total immersion, and the last hope for architecture and the city. He had to shoulder the forbidding aesthetic task, and nothing less than a miracle was asked of him; this labor was not for the fainthearted. As everyone knows, the gamble is paying off and Gehry's building is hailed in article after article as a defining moment in contemporary architecture. Masterpieces are not enough these days, one needs "emblems" (the most recurrent analogy is Sydney's Opera House).

Gehry's apotheosis from major architect to Bilbao savior is also a transformation to a Promethean hero who was spurned at home and who finally vanquished postmodern malaise and recaptured architecture's visionary mission in some grim foreign land better known for industrial decay and terrorist politics. Gehry's pallid titanium artichoke is also meant to fill the gap of the tens of thousand of jobs lost through the demise of the *Altos Hornos*.

At the dawn of the new century, Bilbao is confronted with its greatest historical challenge ever: it must reinvent itself, and the news is that this reinvention is to be accomplished through architecture. In the beginning was architecture ... (see next chapter), and salvation by architecture is the cornerstone of a regenerationist ideology in Bilbao. Once the architect appropriates for himself the mystique of the artist as genius, the building itself becomes far more important than the art within. As Philip Johnson put it, "When a building is as good as that one, fuck the art."

EVERYONE, INCLUDING his detractors, now agree that Gehry is a genius. Gehry complained, "I'm being geniused to death." Sometimes he is lauded as a national treasure but dismissed as a creative artist unable to focus on practical matters, despite his successful application of innovative technologies to architecture. Gehry utilized a three-dimensional computer modeling system, originally designed for the aerospace technology, that turns complex architectural forms into constructable fabrication data and makes his sculptural forms more comprehensible. The computer designs helped hold the colluding, tumbling forms in repose.

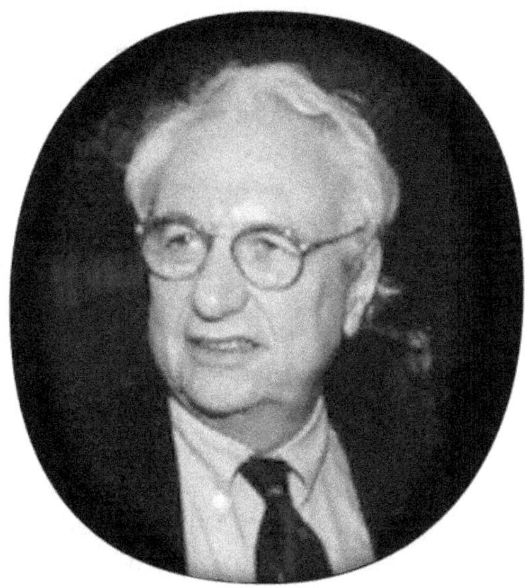

Frank Gehry designed an instant landmark and possibly the most emblematic building of the late twentieth century.
Photo: Iñaki Uriarte.

It has been said so often that it's already a cliché: No other building has had so dramatic an impact on a city since the Sydney Opera House. The startling irregular building is twice as big as the uptown and downtown New York Guggenheims put together (250,000 square feet, with 112,000 of them exhibition space). Although it does not defer to the city's existing architecture, Gehry's building gibes with other aspects of Bilbao, particularly the industrial landscape of Nervión's shipbuilding yards, docks, cranes, and massive, obsolete warehouses. This rich context was cherished by Gehry (see next chapter). He wrote: "To be at the bend of a working river intersected by a large bridge and connecting the urban fabric of a fairly dense city to the river's edge with a place for modern art is my idea of heaven." Seen from the side of the river, the museum evokes a metal ship that has run aground. It's compound curves and great empty center evoke Frank Lloyd Wright's original Guggenheim on Fifth Avenue. "One walks down a long flight of steps into the museum," wrote critic Robert Hughes (*Time*, Nov. 3, 1997), "and the atrium rises—or rather, soars: a large ceremonial space with catwalks and walkways, branching off into galleries at several levels. In it, the three surface types of the museum's construction can be taken in: white sheetrock, plate glass hung on steel members with exaggerated joints and flanges, and titanium skin. (The titanium sounds like an extravagance, but wasn't. Gehry was able to lock up enough of it to cover the museum when the Russians started dumping their stocks of the normally ultraexpensive metal in 1993.) Their forms swelling and deflating in a strongly rhythmical way, large trunks of glass, plaster and titanium rise to the top of the five-story structure; they house utilities, a stair and an elevator.

THE INTENSITY GEHRY can give to a vertical space also transfers to the horizontal ones. The biggest gallery, known as 'the Boat,' is 1.5 times the length of a football field, but with its curved walls and round ceiling trusses, it hasn't a foot of dull space in it. There are a few things in the design that seem arbitrary or merely rhetorical. The towering 'parasol' that Gehry put over the river entrance is pointless except as a visual element—its roof is too high to give any protection from the weather. And the twin stone-veneer towers that rise downstream of the La Salve bridge are just a costly logo. These are quibbles compared with Gehry's achievement in this museum.

"It's a building that spells the end of the smarty-boots, smirkingly facile historicism of which so much Post-modernist building was based—a quoted capital here, an ironic reference there. It isn't afraid of metaphor, but it insists that the essence of building is structure and placemaking. It confronts the rethinking of structure and the formation of space with an impetuous, eccentric confidence. No 'school of Gehry' will come out of it, any more than there could have been a 'school' of Barcelona's Antonio Gaudí. His work is imitation-proof, but liberating."

THE BUILDING HAS become, in its own right, *the* founding work of art of the Bilbao Guggenheim. For the vast majority of the visitors, the museum itself is far more interesting than its contents. Many share Hughes's view about "the dull, inflated conceptual art and late minimalism that appeals to the taste of the Guggenheim's Krens," including, "of course, that one-shot icon of the conformity of late-Modernist official taste, Jeff Koons' *Puppy*, 1992, sitting outside the museum." Hughes concludes, "It would be a tremendous pity if Bilbao ended up with a great building stuffed with heavy-metal, late-imperial American cultural landfill. What broad public is really interested in such art? For the present, however, people will come for the building."

Lesson seventeen

REQUIRED READING

Robert Venturi, Denise S. Brown, and Steven Izenour, Learning from Las Vegas, MIT Press, Cambridge, 1977, 1–72.

Barry Came, "Spain's New Wonder of the World," McLean's, Nov. 1997.

SUGGESTED READING

Rafael Moneo, "Reflecting on Two Concert Halls" (Walter Gropius Lecture, April 25, 1990, Harvard University, Graduate School of Design).

LEARNING GOALS

1. Situate Gehry's architecture within and beyond the modernist / postmodernist paradigms.
2. Get introduced to the significance of Gehry's architecture.
3. Appreciate the uniqueness of the Bilbao Guggenheim building.
4. Can one building transform an entire city? Consider the relationship between architecture and community.

WRITTEN LESSON FOR SUBMISSION

Please write a two- to three-page essay on one of the topics below.

1. Compare and contrast Venturi with Gehry.
2. Describe and comment on the building of the Bilbao Guggenheim.
3. Describe the relationship between the building and the works inside at the Bilbao Guggenheim.
4. Discuss the complex relationship between building and context in Gehry's work in general and in Bilbao in particular.

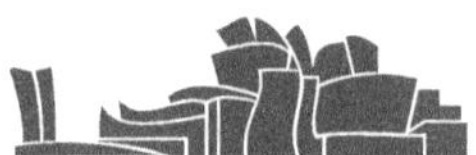

18 · Art / architecture

IN THE BEGINNING was architecture, *arché*. In classical aesthetic theory architecture is the first art. Gehry exemplifies this theory. His Bilbao building overshadows the art within. The building itself has the status of a sculptural work of art that attracts visitors all by itself. Traveling along the Nervión, the shapes and images of the museum emerge and fade depending on viewpoint. It is now a boat, now a castle, a mermaid, an artichoke; its visual language invites metaphor because no concrete description captures the entire object. Image after image, metaphor after metaphor, reminiscence after reminiscence, overlay each other and leave with each viewer a different, but always indelible impression.

Jean-Paul Robert (*L'architecture d'aujourd'hui*, Oct. 1997, 57) wrote, "Seen from any angle, approached from any side, the museum attracts. Its mute masses betray nothing of what they house, but their dancing shapes keep them from being oppressive. Duality is already at work. Some of the shapes are staid, light-coloured, matt, stony. They belong to the city's floor, extending it and its geometry. Their material is telluric. Other shapes are curved, even distorted, covered with raw metal scales. They leap up to the sky. Their cladding has something atmospheric about it. Either its fabrication, which looks rough, reflects the changing moods of the sky, or its metallic character has the strange property of condensing the sky's light, to the point of seeming to irradiate it. Whether skies are grey—as they most often are in the Gulf of Gascony—or fiery as at sunset."

The entrance to the museum is preceded by a wide esplanade of stairs that slip into the atrium. It is a breathtaking atrium of vertical shapes, lifting off in a series of curved forms. The eye follows up the various volumes until they join at their top, while the light diffuses over the surfaces. "The atrium is in movement," writes Robert, "this results from the combination of two oppositions. The first is between top and bottom, between the base, bound by earth and stone to the city, and the volumes suspended in the sky and its light, whose white material is the underside equivalent of the external metal cladding. The second is introduced, plane by plane, by the game of hide-and-seek with the suspended volumes: it brings about an offset with the cardinal directions—the parallel with the river and its perpendicular. Diagonal directions appear, described by the glazed interstices. These gaps of light also have the twin merit of enabling the interior to be projected towards the city and the city to be absorbed by the interior."

IT IS ARCHITECTURE as art in the strongest sense. "The dialectic that produces movement has enabled the inscription of the building in the city, and is masterful to the point of miracle," continues Robert, "but beyond this, it relates and refers to another dialectic, between art and architecture. In the atrium, movements accelerate or slow down thought, as unconsciously as the imperceptible slopes that hasten or hamper steps in the ambulatories. The same thing is at work in the play of framed and unframed views, opacities and openings. All of which, by exercising the eye through architecture, serves to look at art."

Giovannini's piece further explores Gehry's position hovering between art and architecture. His close relationships with American artists is well known and was clearly stimulating. For him, too, forms need not be pure; mastering chaos is the mark of the true artist, and collage can be a valid compositional technique.

Gehry's work goes against the modernist canon, and the beauty of his buildings is not necessarily Euclidean. The normally dominant iconic regularity plays only a supporting role here. Faithful perspective is no longer inviolate and simplicity in impression cedes to complexity in form. It is raw rather than polished. Gehry admits chance and chaos, and intimations of irrationality prove offensive to the modernist spirit. He may take a model from one project and place it in another. He designs by hand rather than head. His decisive contribution is to break the art / architecture barrier, and he doesn't shy away from the mantle of artist. His Bilbao building is a compelling reaffirmation that architecture is indeed the first art.

Lesson eighteen

REQUIRED READING

Michael Sorkin, "Beyond Bilbao," Harper's Bazaar, Dec. 1998.

Allan Schwartzman, "Art vs. Architecture," Architecture, Dec. 1997, 56–59.

SUGGESTED READING

Coosje van Bruggen, "The Origins of the Bilbao Guggenheim" (in Frank O. Gehry: Guggenheim Museum Bilbao, The Salomon R. Guggenheim Foundation, New Tork, 1997, 31–83).

Calvin Tomkins, "The Maverick," The New Yorker, July 7, 1997.

LEARNING GOALS

1. Examine the complex relationship between art and architecture.

---

2. Learn about the history of the Bilbao Guggenheim's construction.
3. Evaluate the architectural splendor of the building from the outside and inside and the building's impact on the city environment.
4. Assess the significance of the Bilbao Guggenheim for the field of architecture.

WRITTEN LESSON FOR SUBMISSION

Please write a two- to three-page essay on one of the topics below.

1. Discuss Gehry's creative process in designing his buildings.
2. Describe the artistic elements in Gehry's masterpiece from the outside and the inside.
3. How has the Bilbao Guggenheim affected the city environment?
4. Comment on the significance of the Bilbao Guggenheim for contemporary architecture.

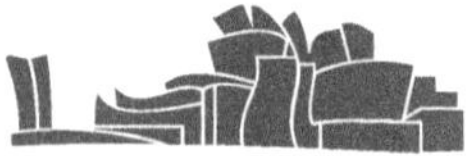

19 · **Tough city**

Gehry's Bilbao Aesthetics

THE SCULPTOR Richard Serra works with large, rusty, twisted steel planks whose heavy metallic shapes with their disturbing imbalance can unsettle any viewer's sense of order. In 1983 he was in Bilbao exhibiting his work along with two other sculptors and three architects when he was overcome by Bilbao's "toughness." He had never seen anything like it! His visual cosmos of rusted, collapsing iron could not find a better resting place than Bilbao, so he called his friend, Frank Gehry, in Santa Monica, California, to discuss of his discovery.

Everything about Bilbao was permeated by an aesthetic of toughness—including the bitter rejection Serra suffered at the hands of Bilbao's officials, who were not only unwilling to buy his work entitled "Bilbao" (done specifically for the city and offered to it for the mere cost of the materials), but unwilling to even take on the danger posed by its seeming instability. The sculpture was dumped into the garden outside Bilbao's Fine Arts museum. It remained there for a year, rejected trash, until a private collector rescued it.

Serra discovered an old, withdrawn Basque sculptor named Jorge Oteiza, quintessentially representative of Bilbao's toughness and himself a victim of public rejection, whose virtually unknown "experimental propositions" and steel "metaphysical boxes" from the 1950s had anticipated later minimalist artists like Serra.

Architect Frank Gehry had been involved in Guggenheim director Thomas Krens's failed Mass MOCA project, the antecedent of the Bilbao Guggenheim. Krens informed Gehry of Bilbao's desire to be a Guggenheim city, and asked him to visit to discuss the project. This exchange reminded Gehry of Serra's enthusiasm and his invitation to visit to Bilbao ten years earlier. Bilbao, the tough city! A month later, Gehry accompanied Krens to Bilbao, stood on the mountain, Archanda, overlooking Bilbao, and saw with his own eyes what Serra had meant. Gehry summed up Bilbao in his now-well-known phrase, "incredible toughness." "Bilbao's beauty resides in its toughness," he said. "I am attracted to industrial hardness in the midst of a green valley." Bilbao, a city with no concessions to mere decorations or pretensions about beauty. A city hard to a sublime fault.

For Serra and Gehry, Bilbao was an exemplar of capitalism's wasteland of industrial ruin and ecological devastation. As artists, they could bridge the frontier between beauty and ugliness, wealth and poverty, glory and ruin. They had the courage to stare at both sides of history and see paradise in hell and beauty in devastation. What could be more emblematic of the global postindustrial, postmodern, and posthumanist world than an entire fabled basin of formerly world-class industries now reduced to ghostly ruins begging to be demolished? There lies the mythology of progress, stripped naked, its truth reduced to allegory.

OTEIZA'S CULTURAL Center (see p. 88) and his aesthetic of ugliness had failed because of its intense political implications. Serra's and Gehry's aesthetics of the tough, viewed and designed from LA / New York's distance, triumphed. First, they had to overcome a considerable obstacle presented by the very artist they planned to exalt. Oteiza had issued a public call for the deaths of those responsible for the American franchise including, of course, Gehry and Serra. This was not a toughness metaphor; this was toughness itself, the metaphor of art driven to its most extreme form, simple, direct action in the real world.

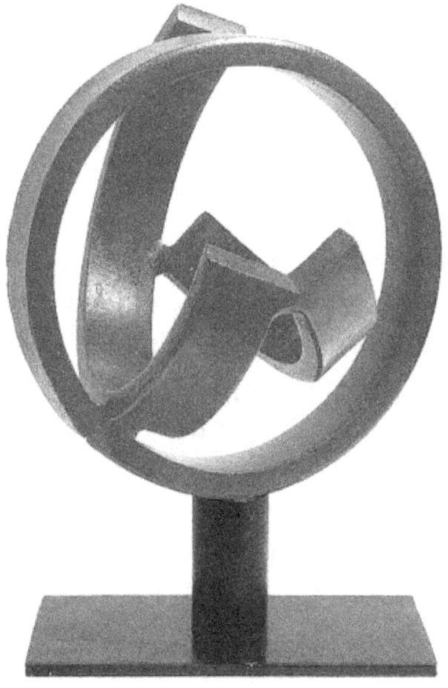

"Disoccupation of the sphere" by Jorge Oteiza.
By permission of the artist.

"Forget writing, stop talking drivel," Oteiza would rail at his interviewers. "Kill them. I will pay you." The Guggenheim's attempts to elevate the man ordering its demolition to the ranks of world-class artist has to rank as another foundational Bilbao paradigm: it is the most audacious instance of cooptation in modern history. Oteiza was begged to sell his work to the Guggenheim as the core of the permanent exhibition. He was unmoved.

The Guggenheim signified the end of the European modernist avant-garde movement, the end of Basque tradition, the end of the artistic revolutionary resistance that he had fathered, nurtured, and kept alive since the 1950s. Oteiza the revolutionary was only interested in brandishing his ultimate weapon, defeat, in the face of the clearly superior firepower of the Guggneheim's money and power to bestow fame.

SERRA AND GEHRY rushed to Bilbao to praise the once-proscribed Oteiza as one of the century's foundational artists. Their proclamation was front-page news. The mostly silenced Oteiza continues his resistance by refusing to allow his work to appear at the Guggenheim unless it is exhibited in the company of other, still ignored Basque artists of his generation.

In any other context, Oteiza would seem like a madman. But in a Basque Country schooled since the 1960s in the ETA's terrorist violence and the overwhelming government reaction, Oteiza's stance fit perfectly. The very week of the opening of the Guggenheim Bilbao, ETA members, attempting to plant a bomb among the flowerpots of Jeff Koons's *Puppy*, were caught by surprise, and killed a security policeman in their escape. In Bilbao the battle over beauty is, beyond metaphor, a matter of life and death. It is, after all, a tough city.

There is continuity between Brecht's ecstatic "How beautiful the moon of Bilbao" and Serra's and Gehry's love affair with the "incredible toughness" of Bilbao. A train ride along the left bank, from Portugalete at the seashore to Abandoibarra in Bilbao's urban center, travels right through the heart of the industrial and urban wasteland. The voyeurism of the vista of kilometers of closed factories and degraded urban centers, still home to 280,000 people, leaves most tourists uncomfortable. But then suddenly—end of the ride, of the tunnel—the marvel of Gehry's voluptuous mermaid of titanium-skinned scales and "metallic flowers" that turn golden at sunset rises over the horizon redemptively. Wow! This apparition at the end of the pilgrimage through the valley of ruins resolves the dialectical tension between such radiant design and its tough urban backdrop. The force field the building creates reverberates through it and the kilometers of ruins preceding it.

One of Gehry's favorite mantras is: "Bilbao has the aesthetics of reality." It is this same "reality" that he has also repeatedly characterized as a "perfect dream" and his "idea of heaven." City officials studiously avoid any analysis of Gehry's enthusiasm for Bilbao's "magic," which has nothing to do with their vision of a beautified, green Bilbao. Cesar Pelli's design for Abandoibarra encompasses the emblematic buildings (the Guggenheim, the Music Hall, and the office tower), as well as a large supermarket and a luxury hotel. Extended areas of parks and gardens make abundant use of interspersed trees and flowerpots. Bilbao's urban planners have produced promotional videos trumpeting plans for large green areas all over the city. Are they dreaming of a Disneyland in Bilbao?

GEHRY, TRAVELING BACK and forth between Los Angeles and Bilbao, knows better than anyone the differences between the two places. The Guggenheim Bilbao and the Disney Concert Hall have recognizable similarities in design, but the fate of the buildings were very different. Whereas Bilbao satisfied him in every respect, Disney was unable to secure financing in Los Angeles, and the project became entangled in a protracted dispute with the architect. For Gehry, the years 1992 to 1997 were bittersweet, marked by the disappointment over the shelved Disney project and the international triumph of Bilbao's "aesthetics of reality." The two designs might bear a close resemblance, but he wants to keep them aesthetically separate, belonging to two utterly different worlds.

In November of 1996 the U.S. pavilion at the VIth Architecture Biennale in Venice (with Thomas Krens as curator) featured work by, among others, Frank Gehry. But Krens and Gehry were not in Venice to tout the spectacular Guggenheim Bilbao Museum, scheduled to open in a few months. Rather, they exhibited the contributions of star architects to Disney projects, Gehry figuring prominently among them. Gehry's association with Disneyland highlights his contrasting insistence upon Bilbao's "aesthetics of reality" and his love affair with the "tough city."

Critics such as John Richardson have characterized Krens's grand projects, his museum franchises in particular, as "shades of Disneyland." But a Disneyfied Bilbao? Neither Gehry nor Krens wish to be perceived as too close to Disney in Bilbao. Gehry wants to make it clear that he knows when he is working in Mickey Mouse's dream world, and when he is working in Bilbao's real world. His "idea of heaven" is the opportunity for his imaginative "metallic flower" to transfigure the abandoned dock lands of a derelict city. It is one thing to use art to create Fantasia beauty for the factory of dreams and spectacle, but is quite another to employ it to transform postindustrial rubble into the tough beauty of a reborn city by means of the power of form and allegory.

NOT THAT BILBAO'S planners are against a Disneyfied spectacle. It is just that the economic logic of postmodern cities is best described as one in which, in John Bird's words, "The urban wasteland has been positioned within the circuits of international finance capital and recorded as a site of consumption and the pursuit of

---

leisure." The process requires an ideology of urban regeneration and gentrification of neighborhoods in decline. The planners wanted to foster a myth of a brand new reality at the waterfront, one firmly situated in the new millennium. The specter of industrial decline and the threat of historical abandonment were mobilized to drive the belief in the new utopian vision of "Bilbao 2000." The real battle is over which map, which representation, which view of the city will prevail. The College of Architecture and City Hall debated for years whether the view of the Guggenheim will or will not be hampered by Pelli's Abandoibarra project. The success or failure of transport policies, architectural decisions, urban design, and emblematic construction plans in the end all hinge on the politics of sight and spectacle.

WILL GEHRY'S "tough city" turn into Gehry's "garden city"? The very thought sickens him. It is one thing to arrive at the unexpected edifice with eyes that have just traveled through the "toughness" of a deserted riverbank, with its ghosts of former docks and shipyards and commercial boats, and to then be swept away by the apparition of a building / whale, a white moon turning into a furnace at dusk, condensing and expanding the various distorted shapes of centuries of industrial struggle. It is quite another to be merely coopted into the emblem of a phony dream of an urban garden next to kilometers of industrial wasteland and presided over by Pelli's central tower. For the magic of "toughness" to work through Gehry's luminous building, it is necessary for the rest of the landscape to specifically *repudiate* any aspirations to the Disneyland dream. Tough beauty is the only beauty worthy of being irradiated by Gehry's building, not a soft, *belle époque* decorative beauty. It makes a world of difference whether his building engages in a dialectical image with the recently-closed,

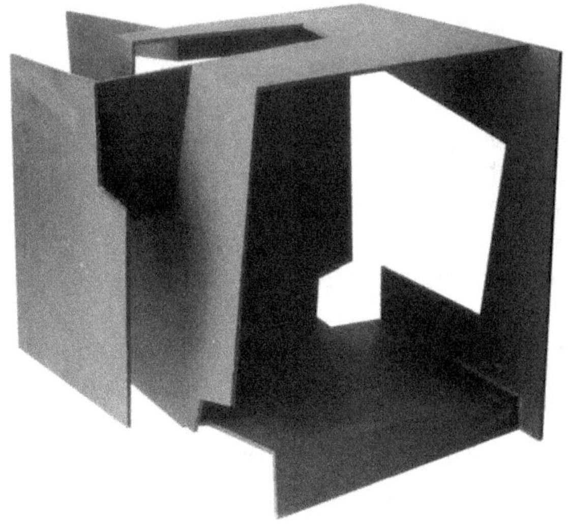

"Portrait of a soldier named Odysseus." From the series "Homage to Mallarmé" by Jorge Oteiza.
By permission of the artist.

imposing Altos Hornos, the lifeblood of thousands of families for a century, or assimilated by Abandoibarra's garden city into a Benetton-like visual shock, provocative, but ultimately in service of selling a new, beautified Bilbao.

"Beauty appears as such only in what is veiled," wrote Benjamin. This essential law of beauty means that Bilbao's true "veil," formed by the hundred smoking chimneys, the omnipresent mantle of debris and grime, the blackness of rivers, is the foundational aspect of its aesthetics. It is second nature to Bilbao, the true face caressed by the region's opaque light and by Brecht's moon. The wonder of Bilbao is not the dust and dirt per se, nor the valleys and buildings, but rather the city wrapped in her industrial veil. It is the secret of her tough beauty.

GEHRY'S BEST-KNOWN building is probably his own house in Santa Monica. It is, in fact, new construction inside an old bungalow, a play of veils, the new wrapped within the old. His Guggenheim is wrapped in its titanium skin, but strives to be connected to Bilbao's "veil" in order to fit naturally within the urban environment. Hence his worry about the new plans for a prettified, softened city. He'd rather maintain the complicity and celebration of Bilbao's harsh veil than see his aesthetics of toughness turn into a mere reflection of the other toughness of Bilbao, its pollution, unemployment, and fierce bureaucracy.

Lesson nineteen

REQUIRED READING

Sheldon Waldrep, "Monuments to Walt" (in The Disney Project, Inside the Mouse: Work and Play at Disney World, Duke University Press, Durham, 1995).

Jon Bird, "Dystopia on the Thames" (in J. Bird, et al., Mapping the Futures, Routledge, 1993).

LEARNING GOALS

1. Understand Bilbao's "tough city" aesthetics of reality
2. Investigate Gehry's and Serra's love for Bilbao aesthetics.
3. Assess the postmodern fascination with the utopian / dystopian confluences in postindustrial cities.

---

4. Examine the continuities and discontinuities between Gehry's work for Disney and for Bilbao.

WRITTEN LESSON FOR SUBMISSION

Please write a two- to three-page essay on one of the topics below.

1. How would you characterize Bilbao's landscapes, industries, buildings, and people?
2. If you were Gehry, traveling back and forth between Los Angeles and Bilbao, how would you describe the differences between the two cities, expressing his particular love for Bilbao?
3. What best typifies Disney aesthetics? Why would or wouldn't that be the appropriate aesthetics for a reinvented Bilbao?
4. From what you have learned of Bilbao's aesthetics, examine critically our common notions about beauty.

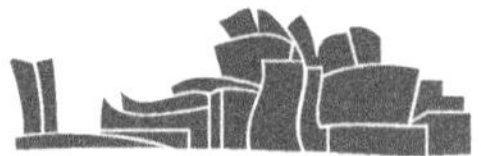

20 · Soft City

Architecture as flagship, spectacle, and ideology

IN THE FINAL analysis, a successful architect is a shaman who can visualize and shape a society's dreams. But he can also be no more than the branded name of a fashionable business, what Calvin Klein is to jeans. The names in the star system of celebrity architects are household words in Bilbao. The architect becomes the savior, and architecture the valued mirror, of the tangible, a crucial ideology of the new urbanism. The discourses of urban regeneration, of cultural industries as essential in economic revitalization, of a new central role for museums and tourism, and of architectural magnificence as the foundation of the transformation of a city's image, become unchallengeable ideological tenets. They must be artfully disseminated and believed. As a byproduct, the architect achieves sainthood.

The past three decades of so-called postmodernism illustrate that architectural canons are the function of concrete discourses as much as concrete buildings. Due to its dependence on public funds, architecture is the site of ideologically warfare more than any other art. Bilbao provides a grand example of architecture as ideology and spectacle. The pretext is the need to create a new postindustrial economy. The fame of the architect serves to sell the product better to the public; some say it can even effect miracles.

The ideological use of architecture is based on the uncontested assumption that public power must invest massively in emblematic buildings by star architects. Emblems, that is, of the ideas of progress, culture, class equality, and peace. The unquestioned premise of architecture as ideology is that once public funds have been invested in architecture, it will equally benefit all social classes.

THE NEW TECHNOLOGIES, the global economy, the tourism industry, and the mass media version of culture have fostered the emphasis on architecture as spectacle. Airports, bridges, museums, and skyscrapers all compete for attention, but is the image of the emblematic building that dominates the creation of public spaces. The Bilbao Guggenheim is the most heavily promoted, and arguably the most successful, emblematic building in the world. These buildings distill the spirit of the times. It is the architectural spectacle that the tourism industry and cities' image-making strategists most value.

In 1996 Luis Fernández-Galiano (*AV Monografias*, 57–58, 212) surmised: "In a world dominated by images, the symbolic meanings traditionally attached to public architecture acquire a mediatic dimension that transcends the limits of space and time. The need for these images to remain recognizable as they get repeatedly reproduced and diffused has caused the author's signature to emerge as yet another asset in the market of symbols, an asset which local government administrations do not hesitate to resort to in their efforts to reassert the importance of their cities in an increasingly competitive world." Illustrative of this process, that very same year (1996), four international architects left their mark in different Spanish cities: Richard Meier in Barcelona designed the Museum of Contemporary Art, Arata Isozaki in La Coruña the Domus Museum, Norman Foster in Bilbao the new metropolitan railway system, and Santiago Calatrava in Valencia the Alameda station and bridge. But even these emblematic buildings were overshadowed the following year by the opening of

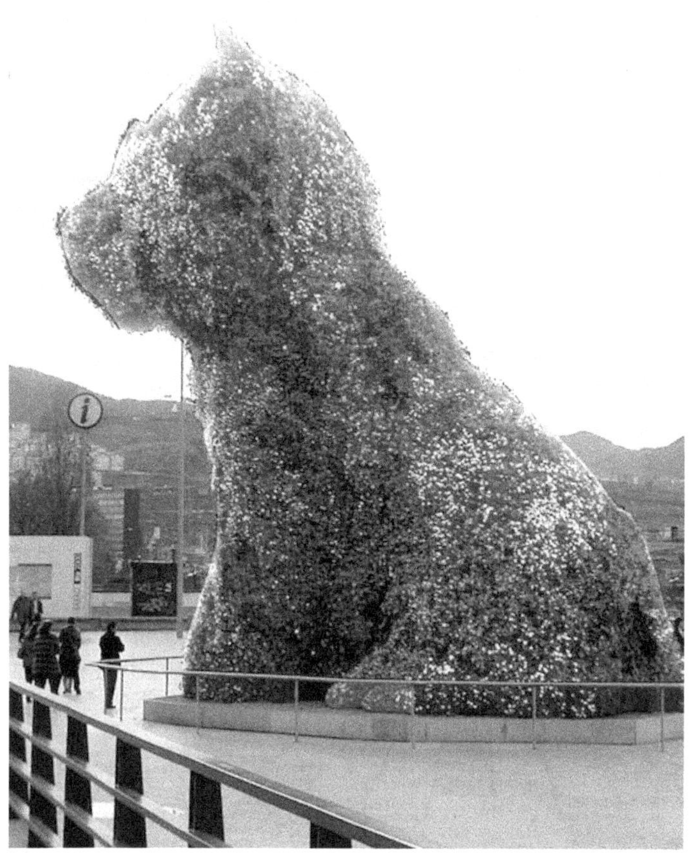

Emblematic works sell a city. Art and achitecture have long served in part as spectacle.
Author's photograph of Jeff Koon's Puppy, *Bilbao.*

---

the Guggenheim in Bilbao and the Getty Center in Los Angeles.

Norman Foster's metro was the first of Bilbao's grand projects and was formidable both technically and architecturally. The project was commissioned to Foster after a public competition. The five-year on-site construction

---

of the first line on the right bank cost about $700 million. A second line on the left bank is being built and is scheduled to be working by the year 2005. The underground metro is a luminous tunnel of glass and stainless steel that creates dazzling effects. The entrances are covered by weightless canopies, and Foster's architectural splendor turns the arteries and intestines of the city into sculptural tunnels of light.

In February 1999 the convention center and music hall, *Euskalduna*, opened its doors to the public in *Abandoibarra*, facing the Guggenheim from the other side of the Deusto Bridge. It was the result of a competition won by the young Madrid architects Federico Soriano and Dolores Palacios. Santiago Calatrava has left his stamp on the city by building the footbridge *Zubizuri* in between the Guggenheim and the town hall (1998), as well as the new airport (2000). The transport hub, initially designed by James Stirling, and later redesigned by Michael Wilford, is still in the planning stages, as is Pelli's urban project for the *Abandoibarra*.

THE LESSON TO learn from Bilbao is that emblematic architecture can be the most powerful tool available to market a city. As examined by Hedley Smyth, flagship developments have become crucial for "selling" a city or an area. They play a high-profile role in promoting urban regeneration and attracting investment. Postmodernism is the cultural context from which to view the significance of such flagship projects. Jonathan Raban describes it perfectly in his *Soft City*: "The city as we imagine it, the soft city of illusion, myth, aspiration, nightmare, is as real, maybe more real, than the hard city one can locate in maps and statistics, in monographs on urban sociology and demography and architecture." Bilbao is poised between the "tough city" celebrated by Gehry's architecture and the "soft city" of futuristic mythology, spectacular voyeurism and "the miracle in Bilbao" literature given authority by his masterpiece. It would be hard to find a more compelling illustration for Bourdieu's proposition that "the most successful ideological effects are those which have no words."

In the end, the fostering of a completely new image becomes essential to all large developmental processes. As subjective as the notion of an overall image of a city is, it can nonetheless be measured in terms of name recognition and tourist appeal; that is, what is captured in the expression "being on the map." Image is not only an abstraction but a product of purposive actions by local officials. It plays a central role in economic development, and its crafting is in fact an arduous process. In brief, we could say that the city as a whole is inaccessible to the imagination unless it can be reduced to a pervasive image.

Lesson twenty

REQUIRED READING

Sharon Zukin, "Disney World: The Power of Façade / The Façade of Power" (in Landscapes of Power: From Detroit to Disney World, University of California Press, Berkeley, 1991).

SUGGESTED READING

Paul Goldberger, "The Politics of Building," The New Yorker, Oct. 21, 1997.

Hedley Smyth, "City Visions and Flagship Developments" (in Marketing the City: The Role of Flagships Developments in Urban Regeneration, E&FN SPON, London, 1994).

LEARNING GOALS

1. Become aware of the "politics of building" being played out by Bilbao officials by means of Gehry's grand architecture.
2. Examine the uses and abuses of architecture as a marketing tool.
3. Understand architecture as spectacle and as myth.
4. Assess the ideological function of salvation by architecture.

WRITTEN LESSON FOR SUBMISSION

Please write a two- to three-page essay on one of the topics below.

1. What are flagship developments, and what role does architecture play in them?
2. Describe the postmodern cultural context in which architecture turns into pure spectacle.
3. Analyze the ideological dimension of architecture in promoting urban redevelopment, social cohesion, and the idea of progress.
4. How would you play dialectically with the alleged aesthetic opposites of "tough city" and "soft city"?
5. Is image central to urban development processes?

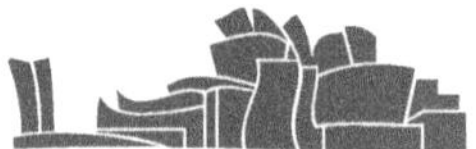

21 · **Museums**

Temples, forums, or theme parks?

THE MUSEUMS ARE in desperate need of psychotherapy," wrote Duncan Cameron in 1972. "There is abundant evidence of an identity crisis in some of the major institutions while others are in an advanced state of schizophrenia."

During the 1980s the museum became a privileged institution in the hands of postmodern writers. James Clifford described the history of French ethnography between the two world wars, for example, as "a tale of two museums." The Trocadéro and the new Musée de L'Homme exerted major ideological and practical influences on the course of anthropological research. For those who see culture and its norms as artificial arrangements readily exchangeable with other possible dispositions, the museum is an excellent laboratory for viewing alternate cultural representations. It was in the jumble of exotica of the Trocadéro that Picasso discovered African art. As the enthusiasm for things primitive blossomed, the scandalous ethnographic museum turned into a museum of art.

During the 1990s the museum as an institution was to be confronted with the historical novelty of Krens's franchised transnational museum in Bilbao. Krens's invention deserves close scrutiny. The willingness of the Basques, renowned for the mystery of their isolated language and other ethnographic exotica, to let the politics of their artistic identity be determined by a New York museum curator is remarkable. The contradiction and complicity between ethnographic primitivists and avant-garde modernists, between an artistic mainstream in need of funds and a subaltern periphery in need of recognition, has fascinating implications for museology, anthropology, and the international commodification of art and culture. Some of the problems that deserve close attention are the function of museums, the accommodations of the art market, the nature of art, and the relations between international and local artists. The anti-museum movement of the 1960s and 1970s wrote the museum canon of the 1990s; the manufacturing and selling of national identities and avant-garde movements were the politics of cultural representation.

A BASIC PREMISE of all museum exhibits is that they inevitably draw on the cultural assumptions of the people who produce them. Some elements are emphasized and others are downplayed. Any exhibit therefore takes place in a contested arena of cultural representations and resources. The very question of the necessity for a Guggenheim-type museum was heavily contested when it was first proposed.

Anthropologists in particular are most aware of the extent to which, as Lavine and Karp put it, "Decisions about how cultures are presented reflect deeper judgments of power and authority and can, indeed, resolve themselves into claims about what a nation is or ought to be as well as how citizens should relate to one another." Visits to universal survey museums such as the Louvre, the El Prado, or the Metropolitan Museum of Art, on the other hand, functions for many as rituals of citizenship, and establish the canon of what constitutes civilization itself. Such museums, with their architectural and art-historical claims, represent society's classical heritage, and play a major role in legitimizing the modern state.

Duncan Cameron distinguishes between the traditional function of the museum as temple and the newer one of the museum as cultural forum. As a temple, a museum has a "timeless and universal function, the use

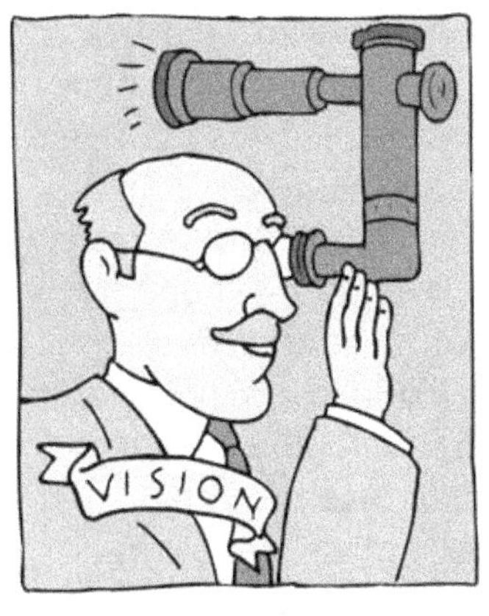

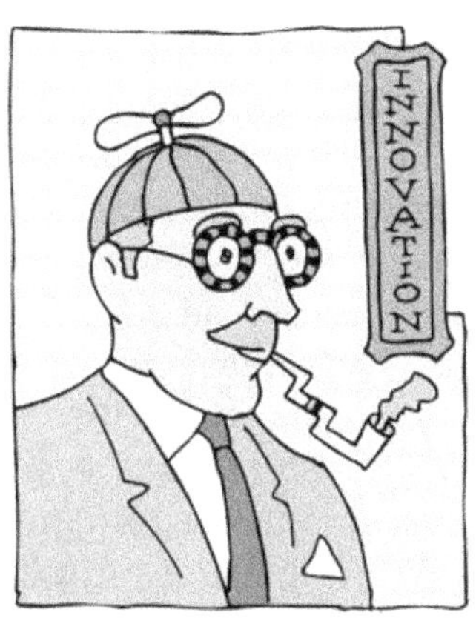

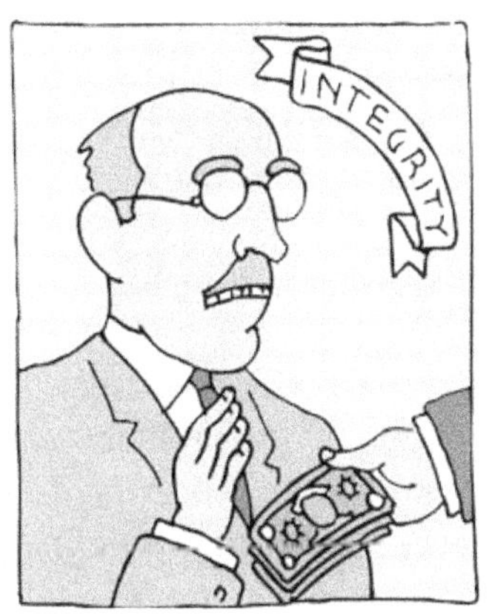

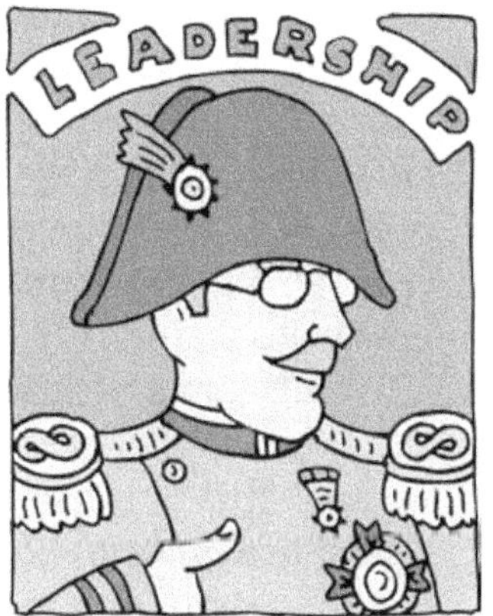

Museums can become the showcase for the people who run them.
Illustration: Seymour Chwast

---

of a structured sample of reality, not just as a reference but as an objective model against which to compare individual perception." As forum, the museum is a place for "confrontation, experimentation and debate." Some modified version of universalist aesthetics still applies to art museums, even if curators are well aware that their points of view are only not the only possible ones. The temple / forum distinction leads us to more appropriate historical analogies for the newest museums in which visitors are confronted with shops, restaurants, performances, and lectures. A fair? A shopping mall? A theme park? An entertainment center.

VICTORIA NEWHOUSE, in her *Toward a New Museum* (The Monacelli Press, New York, 1998), classified museums according to these categories:

1. "The cabinet of curiosities": Art museums based on private collections that were assembled long before those public institutions came into being.
2. "The museum as sacred space": Specialized museums with a didactic approach, under the strong belief in art's ability to improve humankind, and with a sense of public entitlement to culture.
3. "The monographic museum": A museum that enshrines an individual artist.
4. "The museum as subject matter: Artists' museums and their alternative spaces": Extensions to their work created by artists.
5. "The museum as entertainment": Museums as vehicles for entertainment à la Disneyland.
6. "The museum as environmental art": When architecture becomes an active container that foregrounds its artistic content.

The Bilbao Guggenheim is the most obvious model of the museum as environmental art. It has been hailed as "the" museum of the turn of the century. On the other hand, Krens's museum project for Bilbao has substantial elements of the museum as entertainment as well.

Krens defined the art museum as "a theme park with four attractions: good architecture, a good permanent collection, primary and secondary art exhibitions, and amenities such as shops and restaurants" (quoted in V. Newhouse, *Towards a New Museum,* 191). (See chapter twenty on the theme-park aspect of the Bilbao Guggenheim.)

WRITING ON THE relationship between art and ethnicity, Beardsley and Livingston ("The Poetics and Politics of Hispanic Art: A New Perspective" in *Exhibiting Cultures*) directly challenge the entrenched idea that as an artist approaches the realm of high art, elements of ethnicity inevitably disappear. "Ethnicity, along with other forms of regional or cultural particularity, can now be perceived as one of the primary ingredients in the alchemy that is good art." Beardsley's and Livingston's thoughts were inspired by the 1987 "Hispanic Art in the United States" exhibition, which received an enthusiastic but controversial reception from critics. Their central point is that the question of this relationship should itself provoke multiple and conflicting responses from curators and viewers, because of their differing cultural perspectives.

In the introduction to their standard reader, *Exhibiting Cultures*, Lavine and Karp conclude: "The museum world needs movement in at least three arenas: (1) the strengthening of institutions that give populations a chance to exert control over the way they are presented in museums; (2) the expansion of the expertise of established museums in the presentation of non-Western cultures and minority cultures in the United States; and (3) experiments with exhibition design that will allow museums to offer multiple perspectives or to reveal the tendentiousness of the approach taken."

It is worth remembering these issues of culture and representation in order to assess the magnitude of the changes wrought by the Bilbao Guggenheim. Krens's piece argues that "the most vital function that a museum can provide ... is its capacity to give space to seduction of incongruity." Under his direction, the exhibit of motorcycle models has been the most popular one at the Bilbao Guggenheim. If previously the question of who controlled the institutional and curatorial aspects of an exhibit was an object of struggle, no such concerns matter in Bilbao where Krens, living on the other side of the Atlantic, is directly in charge of all artistic purchases, exhibits, and curatorial decisions.

THIS NEW MUSEUM phase has to be judged in the context of the eclectic, postmodern "imaginary museum," well suited to attract large amounts of tourists, according to Krens. The whole of humanity becomes an imaginary museum, and "there is a growing awareness that postmodernity is a special case, for it welcomes a virtually infinite interaction of relationships between, among, and within the various scientific, natural, economic, political, cultural and social discourses that make up our universe and its fields of enquiry." Such postmodernism is an outgrowth of metropolitan-centered processes. In critic Fredric Jameson's expression, it is the cultural dominant of late capitalism which points to a crisis of cultural authority in the Western European culture and its institutions.

Lesson twenty-one

REQUIRED READING

Duncan Cameron, "The Museum: A Temple or the Forum," Journal of World History, 14(1): 191–202.

Ivan Karp, "Culture and Representation." (in I. Karp and S. Lavine, Exhibiting Cultures: The Poetics and Politics of Museum Display, Smithsonian Institution, 1991, 11–24)

SUGGESTED READING

Thomas Krens, "Museums and History: The Dynamics of Culture in a Postmodern Era" (in The Guggenheim Museum Salzburg. A Project by Hans Hollein. The Salomon Guggenheim Foundation, Salzburg, 1990, 53–61).

LEARNING GOALS

1. Explore the debates concerning the role of the museum.
2. Examine the relationship of the museum with the rest of the culture as representation.
3. Understand the historical novelty of the Bilbao Guggenheim Museum.
4. Assess the significance of museums in postmodern thinking.

WRITTEN LESSON FOR SUBMISSION

Please write a two- to three-page essay on one of the topics below.

1. Apply a variety of historical analogies to a variety of museums.
2. Should culture and representation issues be raised vis-à-vis the Bilbao Guggenheim. Could this one museum determine for the global art world what Clif-

ford claims two museums did for French ethnography between the great wars?

3. Is the Bilbao Guggenheim "modernist," "postmodernist," or something else?
4. Is the Bilbao Guggenheim a historical novelty? Why or why not?

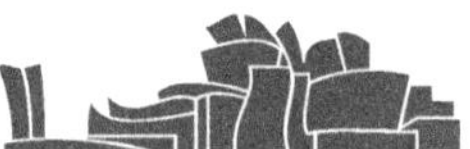

22 · Museum culture

Commodity fetishism, and the Benetton Effect

THE BILBAO GUGGENHEIM is part of an explosion of new museums worldwide. Five thousand museums have sites on the Internet and, in the United States alone, 600 new art museums have opened since 1970. During Mitterrand's fourteen years in power (until 1995), 400 museums were built or renovated in France. Bilbao is a grand example of the attention a museum can receive from the media as well as from art critics and the scholarly community. Whether in terms of architecture, art exhibits, urban renewal flagships, the nationalist politics of building, the transnational museum experiment, or the contrast between local and global narratives, Bilbao has occupied a prominent place in the international media and in artistic and architectural publications.

From a scholarly viewpoint, the complexity of the issues raised by the creation of the Bilbao Guggenheim forces us to view the museum, in Sherman and Rogoff's summary, as an "intricate amalgam of historical structures and narratives, practices and strategies of display, and the concerns and imperatives of various governing ideologies" (*Museum Culture*, ix). Museums are strategic sites for an inquiry into modes of cultural construction.

Sherman's essay examines the history of critical discourse about museums, from Quatremère (French Revolution) and Marx to Benjamin and recent work. It questions received history by reinscribing these discourses into concepts such as fiction, desire, consciousness, representation, and fetishism. These expanded histories invoke Foucault's insistence on the primacy of the relationship between epistemic structures, disciplinary boundaries, the construction of internally coherent discourses, and the play of power relations.

BILBAO'S GUGGENHEIM has become a paradigm for the power of a single building to instigate urban renewal and perform an architectural "miracle." What has made it such a success is the interplay of innovative design, the application of computer technology, the politics of building, the significance of architecture in city transformations, tourist economy, and critical acclaim. The "Guggenheim Effect" has social and intellectual consequences that have transformed the museum as an institution and legitimized the politics of weighing the pros and cons of large gambles. These consequences include widening the audience for Guggenheim collections and American art, turning architecture into the paramount artistic expression of cities, and attracting hordes of tourists to a reinvented Bilbao. They are, quite simply, historic.

The seemingly innocuous concept of "the public" conceals deep ambiguities. The museological context exists within a larger signifying process that invokes notions of community. In order to fulfill its social function, a museum constructs an entity to address itself to: the viewer, or in collective terms, the public. What is this "public" that the Guggenheim is serving? How is the museum transforming Bilbao's sense of self as a city? How is this "the public" addressed by a museum related to the larger museum-going international public? According to Sherman and Rogoff, "museums can serve as a site for the construction of fictitious histories that respond to unconscious desires." The term "museal" refers to dead realities, and "strategies of display can make museums the funerary sites for uncomfortable or inconvenient historical narratives." They can serve as an "architecture of amnesia" that will attempt to erase the industrial and urban histories that anteceded the new splendorous building.

PROMOTIONAL CULTURE is another aspect of postmodern aesthetics which museums exploit. These aesthetics, at the intersection of advertisement and commerce, of politics and representational pedagogy, are perhaps best illustrated by the "united colors of Benetton." Thanks to the skillful technique and discourse of photographer Oliviero Toscani, images that shocked people in the past have become "the most effective way of selling commodities today." Such discourses emphasize the politics of representation and the representation of politics. They may include a terrorist car bombing, AIDS, inmates on death row, racism, or war atrocities. In such aesthetics, the relationships between identity formation, commerce, pedagogy, and politics are reworked. The technique consists simply in shocking the viewer with provocative photographs in order to fix the name "Benetton" in their minds and then rip off the commercial benefits of successful advertisement (in 1991 alone Benetton's stock rose 24 percent). Such banal use of socially pressing issues such as racism, war, prisons, children's rights, and natural catastrophes to foster consumption has been subject to severe criticism. Benetton's reply accuses its critics of censorship. By seizing the controversy to identify themselves as a force for social responsibility, Benetton links its name to ideology in the form of books, interviews, talks and star endorsements. Their theme in brief, according to Giroux, is: "Benetton is not about selling sweaters but social responsibility, and it is a company that represents less a product than a lifestyle and worldview." What is significant about the Benetton strategy is the use of postmodern culture of diversity and social responsibility

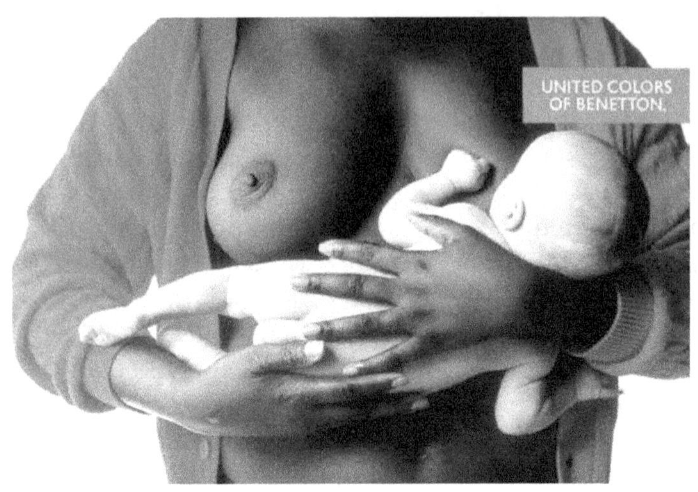

The Benetton technique shocks the viewer with a provocative photograph in order to fix a trademark in his mind.
Photo: Oliviero Toscani, courtesy of the Benetton Group.

---

for promotion and profit making, commodifying human tragedy with an eye on the commercial imperatives of brand recognition. The owner, Luciano Benetton, has no doubt that the bottom line is profit, not social justice. But the director of communication, Peter Fresola, insists that Benetton is really interested in art with a social image, that is, an image that will change people's minds and create compassion. Toscani appeals to the high moral ground by separating his economic role as the director of advertisement from the process itself of communication that he suggests is untarnished by commercialism.

Benetton has become a corporate model for post-Fordist production. They provide less security, fewer benefits, lower wages, and there is less state presence. Since capital has fallen in love with cultural difference, what matters now is the deft combination of commercial success, ideological legitimization, and adaptation to the changing economy and culture of post-Fordism. This might require the use of great art and photography, as well as the cynical use of the discourse of social justice, always for the ultimate goal of making profit.

POSTMODERN CULTURE (see chapter twenty-three) faces the dilemma of maintaining particularity while fitting into a global economy. Postmodern culture projects representations that affirm the value of difference while denying the existence of real differences. The difference affirmed is stripped of all social and political antagonism and becomes a mere commercial marker for what is hip and fashionable. In this logic of the spectacle and the selling of fantasies, all distinctions between news, advertising, editorials, public events, and feature stories break down. By using shock, sensationalism, and voyeurism, Giroux argues, the Benetton images are "offering the company's publicity mechanisms to diverse cultures as a unifying discourse for solving the great number of social problems that threaten to uproot difference from the discourse of harmony, consensus, and fashion."

Museums such as the Bilbao Guggenheim are deeply enmeshed in this postmodern promotional culture. The Guggenheim's director, Thomas Krens, defined the art museum as "a theme park" (see chapter twenty-one). Some of Krens's exhibits, such as the one devoted to motorcycle models (sponsored by BMW), and the incoming Armani suits ($15 million in support from Armani), follow the Benetton paradigm of putting great art, architecture, photography, and design, in combination with the discourses of socio-economic responsibility and urban renewal, to use in a promotional strategy whose ultimate goal is the attraction of large crowds for the sake of the institution's and the city's name recognition, power, and money. They raise large questions about the boundaries between art and promotional venture.

THE IDENTITY DEBATES between "Basque" art and "universal" art need to be situated in the context of the politics of representation and the culture of consumption. "Culture is increasingly constituted by commerce," Giroux observes, "and the penetration of commodity culture into every facet of daily life has become the major axis of relations of exchange through which corporations actively produce new, increasingly effective forms of address." It is not that such consumerism is a form of domination, or to a lesser degree, some form of cultural imperialism from afar, but, "what is at stake in the new intersection of commerce, advertising, and consumption is the very definition and survival of public cultures." If these cultures are to thrive, open and democratic processes must provide for a problematization of the intersection of power and representation, recognition of the political and pedagogical limits of consumerism, and allowance for the resurgence of truly multicultural identities.

Lesson twenty-two

REQUIRED READING

Daniel Sherman, "Quatremère / Benjamin / Marx: Art Museums, Aura, and Commodity Fetishism" (in D. Sherman and I. Rogoff, Museum Culture: Histories,

Discourses, Spectacles, University of Minnesota Press, Minneapolis, 1994).
Henry A. Giroux, "Consuming Social Change: The United Colors of Benetton" (in H. Giroux, Disturbing Pleasures: Learning Popular Culture, Routledge, New York, 1994).

LEARNING GOALS

1. Examine the history of critical discourse about the museum as an institution.
2. Understand museum culture and the larger context of the community.
3. Evaluate museums, promotional culture, and commodity fetishism.
4. Assess Benetton as the corporate model for post-Fordist production that uses postmodern strategies of good art and the discourse of social responsibility to achieve increasing profits.

WRITTEN LESSON FOR SUBMISSION

Please write a two- to three-page essay on one of the topics below.

1. What is the role of a critical discourse, if any, in confronting the case of the Bilbao Guggenheim's success?
2. Do you perceive any "Benetton effect" in Bilbao?
3. Discuss the various ways in which "museum culture" is central to Bilbao's global transformation.
4. Which public is the Bilbao museum serving?

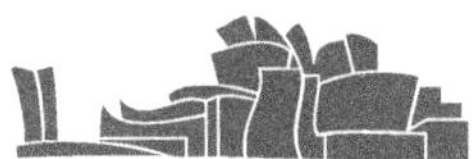

23 · The global postmodern space

POSTMODERNITY ENTAILS a variety of cultural and social changes that are taking place in contemporary advanced societies. Postmodernism emerged as an intellectual movement during the 1970s. The ambiguous use of the term is due to the multiplicity of its definitions and the heterogeneity of the factors involved. Philosophy, social sciences, art, architecture, literature, to name a few, have been enormously influenced by the postmodern paradigm.

Modernity was the child of the eighteenth-century Enlightenment. A basic assumption of enlightened modernity was the belief that the world is a coherent whole. Linear progress, the search for objective knowledge and truth, and the use of social-scientific knowledge for rational planning and the reconstruction of society were part of the modernist agenda. Theorists such as Marx, Max Weber, Durkheim, Freud, and others provided compelling analyses as well as forceful moral critiques of modern society. They sought to explain the social conditions, contradictions, and changes taking place in their societies. The French Revolution and the economic changes brought about by the industrial revolution were the main elements in modernist analyses of social disorder and change in capitalist societies. The theories vary considerably, but they all share the notion that the world can be rationally analyzed and improved.

Modernist analysis of the city has in particular emphasized this belief in rational organization. The modern city combined sites of production, administration, capital circulation and consumption. Simmel and other writers viewed the city as the essential locale for the formation of modernity. The city became a symbol for modernity and was the site of progress and the development of social order.

Postmodernists are skeptical of the idea of unilinear progress. Fragmentation, indeterminacy, pluralism, chaos, ephemerality, discontinuity, and relativism are the salient traits of postmodern thinking. Collage has become the signature postmodern style, and it has become harder than ever before to grasp any scientific, objective truth by which to interpret the world. As Lyon puts it, "Today's more general acceptance of the view that our observations depend on assumptions, and that those assumptions are connected with world-views and with power positions makes relativity, not to say relativism, seem more natural." Science itself becomes another "language game." Since no theoretical argument can claim objective validity or intellectual superiority, the only possibility is to "deconstruct" it, or critically examine its fundamental elements, assumptions, and historical contexts.

MANY SOCIAL scientists have judged such extreme relativism negatively. Harvey, for example, in (*The Condition of Postmodernity*, Blackwell, Oxford, 1989, 116) wrote of postmodernism's "penchant for deconstruction bordering on nihilism, its preference for aesthetics over ethics [which] takes matters too far. ... Postmodernist philosophers tell us not only to accept but even to revel in the fragmentation and the cacophony of voices through which the dilemmas of the modern world are understood. Obsessed with deconstructing and delegitimizing every form of argument they encounter, they can end only in condemning their own validity claims to the point where nothing remains of any basis for reasoned action." Harvey argues that the dynamic character of capitalism as a mode of economic production and technological revolution has eliminated time-space restrictions. Through a computer-equipped modern technology, information of any databank can be accessed immediately. Without space / time coordinates to geographically fix languages of everyday life, social control becomes a major problem for the dominant groups. Postmodernists believe that, together with the emergence of electronically mediated languages, new forms of power have emerged, eluding concepts such as tyranny or alienation.

THE CONDITIONS OF postmodernity have been enormously influenced by the explosion of consumerism. Life has become commodified, everything is reduced to exchange value, and commodities do not represent the results of production. Fashion and style are better terms to determine value, and consumption has become the main vehicle for personal satisfaction. Competition and individual success have become far more important than principles of solidarity. Advertis-ing has invaded everything and consumerism seems to neutralize any criticism of the status quo.

The massive extension of technological advances and the mass media have decisively contributed to the emergence of the contemporary consumer society. Television has achieved a central position in society and has turned into its cultural epicenter. According to Castells, the strength of television is grounded in its capacity to "set the stage for all processes that intend to be communicated to the society at large, from politics to business, including sports and arts." (*The Rise of the Network Society*, Blackwell, Oxford, 1996, 336). This means that messages that are not recognized by the media eventually end up disappearing from the collective mind.

Mass media creates a "virtual reality" in which factual and symbolic representations are collapsed. Life is conceived in terms of show and spectacle, "simulacra," in

---

Baudrillard's terminology. Simulation is communicated as real and the imaginary and the real become one. Such "hyper-reality" mobilizes subjects in the postmodern world. Baudrillard's words are typical of postmodernist jargon: "It is reality itself today that is hyperrealist. Surrealism's secret already was that the most banal reality could become surreal, but only in certain privileged moments that are still nevertheless connected with art and imagery. It is quotidian reality in its entirety—political, social, historical, and economic—that from now on incorporates the simulatory dimension of hyperrealism. We live everywhere already in an 'aesthetic' hallucination of reality."

Postmodern lifestyles are described in terms of "eclecticism," where everything appears to be mixed and boundaries have almost disappeared. The separation of the so-called high and mass cultures gets elided. If it sells, it is right. Everything is valid in the postmodern culture of late capitalism.

THE SERVICE CLASS—that is, those who control the use of culture, information, and access to the organization bureaucracy—has become the dominant class in the capitalist economy. Moreover, in postmodern thinking the emergence of the service class implies the end of class struggle between capitalists and the industrial working class. The goal for workers is not the control of the production system, but, instead, the establishment of the working class establishes as a client of the State engaged in distributional competition with employers. Thereby, the service class cannot be seen as a Marxist "class-for-itself," with a sense of a community sharing the same interests, nor can it be seen as a dominant class, because its members do not own the means of production. Class identity no longer represents an

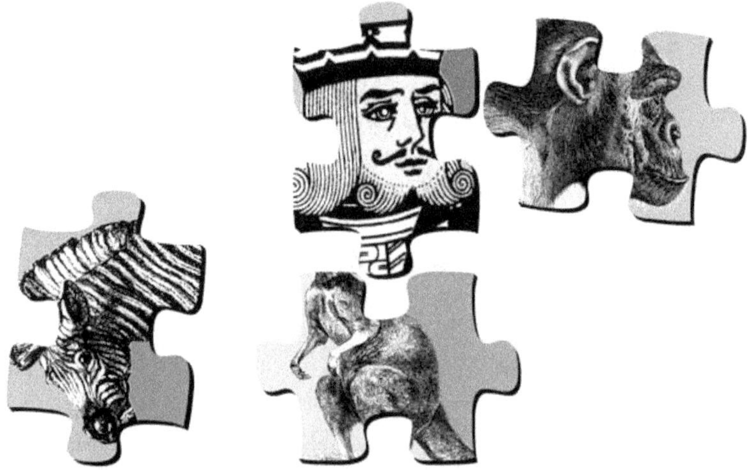

Fragmentation, indeterminacy, chaos, ephemerality, discontinuity and relativism are defining elements of postmodern thinking. Assembling the pieces is a work in progress.

---

integrated and self-conscious character. Class domination is multidimensional, global, and strongly abstract. Class identity is a very complex entity in today's global capitalist system. The goal of humanity now seems to be consumption, independent of any social stratification.

The adoption of postmodern ideas by cities has powerful consequences for urban planning. According to Harvey, the postmodern idea of planning does not necessarily take social objectives into consideration: "Aesthetics has triumphed over ethics as a prime focus of social and intellectual concern." The modern idea of planning and development as large scale, metropolitan-wide, technologically rational, and efficient has disappeared with the advent of postmodernism. Space has a different meaning for modernists and postmodernists. Whereas the former conceives of space as an element to be molded in order to achieve social purposes, the latter perceives space only in terms of aesthetics and beauty. Urban planning has abandoned the search for uniformity and equality in the modern city. Instead, the spectacular postmodern architecture that shapes cities today believes in anesthetization and imagery. The postmodern city has become a place for spectacle, consumption, and worldwide corporate decision-making. In these cities, advertising and conspicuous acts of consumption are all that count.

Lesson twenty-three

REQUIRED READING

Stuart Hall, "The Local and the Global: Globalization and Ethnicity" (in A. McClintock, A. Mufti and E. Shoat, Dangerous Liaisons, University of Minnesota Press, Minneapolis, 1997, 173–187).

SUGGESTED READING

David Lyon, "From Postindustrialism to Postmodernity" (in D. Lyon, Postmodernity, Univ. of Minnesota Press, Minneapolis, 1994, 37–53).

LEARNING GOALS

1. Basic premises of the postmodern paradigm.
2. The relationship of postmodernism to postindustrialism, informational economies and consumerism.
3. The effects of the postmodern condition on issues of identity and politics.
4. The dynamics of globalization over issues of ethnicity.

WRITTEN LESSON FOR SUBMISSION

Please write a two- to three-page essay on one of the topics below.

1. What does postmodernism entail socially, culturally, politically, and intellectually?
2. What elements characterize a postmodern lifestyle?
3. What consequences have resulted from the hegemony of postmodern ideas in city planning?
4. How does globalization affect ethnicity?

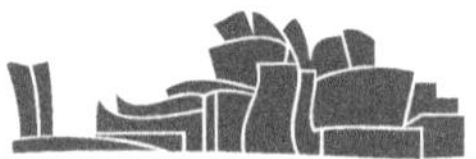

24 · Selling Bilbao

The political economy of space and identity

USUALLY WE CONCEIVE of a culture as the property of people in a specific location. Anthropologists need to go to the place to study it, but, increasingly, cultural difference is being deterritorialized. Migration, transnational culture, financial flow, and postcolonial realities force on us new approaches to the specialization of national differences and cultural identities. According to Akhil Gupta and James Ferguson, "The larger point is not simply the claim that cultures are no longer (were they ever?) fixed in place. Rather, the point, well acknowledged but worth restating, is that all association of place, people, and culture are social and historical creations to be explained, not given natural facts." (*Culture, Power, Place*, Duke University, Durham, 1997, 4).

Another established notion in Western thought is the idea of culture as order. Under the label "poststructuralism," authors like Foucault have insisted on the centrality of power relations at all social levels. The emphasis is on the active practices of social agents and the ways they reappropriate culture and place, not simply to enact, but to transmit and inhabit them. Thinkers such as Raymond Williams and Stuart Hall have concentrated on the contingent, incomplete nature of all cultural hegemonies. Any political field is a contested one; any subject position is in battle with alternative positions.

The practices of place-making deserve special attention once we challenge the notions of culture and politics as spatially territorialized. Bilbao's history, which we examined during the first chapters of this book, provides a good example of how locality and community are politically and discursively constructed. We saw in those chapters how local, regional, and global economies were interdependent. We need to ask now how our understandings of locality, community, and the idea of a global space are formed and experienced.

In the interplay between the local and the global there is always the danger of overvaluing "the origins" as the natural and motherly place to which one is constantly returning. But supralocal identities need not be mere spatial and temporal extensions of such natural identities, rooted in ideas of a primordial community with gender associations of the local with domesticity, women, and a private space.

BILBAO ILLUSTRATES the close relationship between place-making and identity. The elusive notion of "identity" allows for very different political projects and analytic strategies. It is worth recalling Stuart Hall 's idea that identities are not essential entities of stable continuity, but are better conceived as "meeting points" of temporary identification that allow the subject to act. Akhil and Ferguson wrote: "Discussions of identity, it seems to us, all too easily fall into the model of possession and ownership embodied in discourses about the sovereign subject: an identity is something that one 'has' and can manipulate, that one can 'choose;' or, inversely, it is something that acts as a source of 'constraint' upon the individual, as an ascribed rather than a chosen feature of life. In both cases, the individual subject is taken as a pre-given entity, identities as the many masks or cages it may inhabit. Such positions are perfectly compatible with the observation that identities (like the contents of 'cultures' themselves) are historically contingent. But what is missing from such a conception is the crucial insight that the subject is not simply affected by changing schemes of categorization and discourses of difference but is actually constituted or interpolated by them."

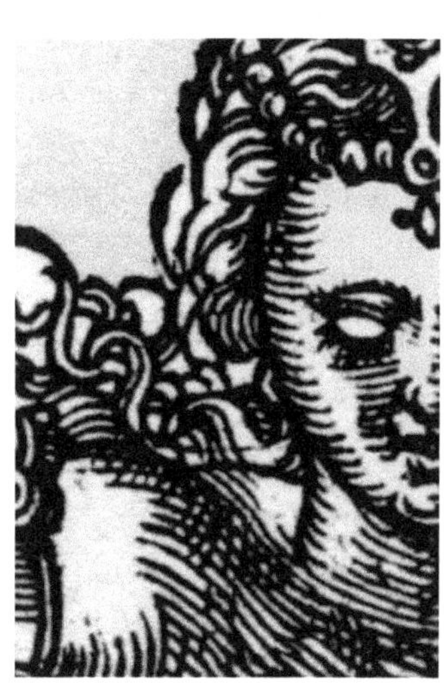
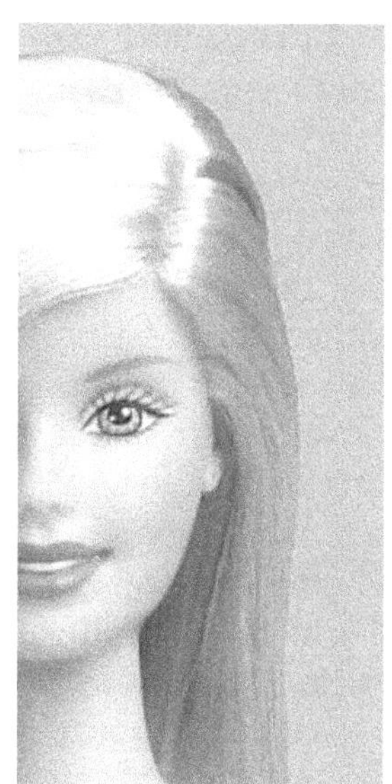

In modern times, few cities have attempted a change of identity more striking than Bilbao. It has been an extraordinary success.
Left: detail of woodcut by Jost Amman. Right: Barbie, one of the most popular dolls of all time.

PLACE-MAKING IS not simply the discovery of a natural locality; it involves construction. Similarly, identity is a mobile relation of difference rather than the outgrowth of a rooted community. In the dialectics of place and community, the notions of identity and alterability are simultaneously produced. The other major theme in such formations is resistance. Resistance adopts its forms in the struggle with the changing mechanisms of power, but exists only in relation to those mechanisms. The practices of resistance are themselves never innocent of nor outside of power. They are always tainted by co-optation, complicity, and the adoption, unintentionally ironic, of former stances of resistance within new strategies of power. The widespread initial resistance to the Guggenheim Museum in Bilbao, and the corresponding shifting and changing of positions later, demonstrates the role of resistance in the process of place-making and identity transformation.

In Harvey's essay about the dynamics of place and space in the postmodern condition, he finds "place" to be one of the most multilayered and multipurpose words in the language. Some words refer to the generic qualities of place (locality, locale, neighborhood, region, and territory), others designate particular kinds of places (city, village, town, metropolis, or state), and still others have strong connotations of place (home, hearth, community, nation, and landscape). "Place" has an extraordinary range of metaphorical meanings. Harvey addresses the issue of why the elaboration of place-bound identities has become more rather than less important in the present globalized world. He finds that space relations have been restructured since the 1970s in the totalizing spread of global capital accumulation.

BILBAO IS A city that once had a secure status, but precipitously found itself, in the early 1980s, in a very vulnerable economic and social position. In the competition for highly mobile capital increasingly sensitive to the qualities of places, postindustrial, ruin-strewn Bilbao found itself gravely threatened. Few cities would have a more difficult job in selling themselves than Bilbao. This led to speculative attempts to create place, including the flagship architecture strategy. Harvey on the ongoing process in Bilbao: "Interplace competition is not simply about attracting production, however. It is also about attracting consumers through the creation of a cultural center, a pleasing urban or regional landscape, and the like. Investment in consumption spectacles, the selling of images of places, competition over the definition of cultural and symbolic capital, the revival of vernacular traditions associated with places, all become conflated in interplace competition. I note in passing that much of postmodern production in, for example, the realism of architecture and urban design, is precisely about the selling of place as part and parcel of an ever-deepening commodity culture."

ALL OF THIS LEADS to the battles over representation by cities in need of changing their images. Bilbao's extraordinary success relies in great part on such cultural politics of place-making, of putting the city "on the map," of using the social power associated with its historically industrious and adventurous character, and of masterfully deploying a political economy of place and identity.

Lesson twenty-four

REQUIRED READING

David Harvey, "From Space to Place and Back Again: Reflections on the Condition of Postmodernity" (in J. Bird, et al. Mapping the Futures, Routledge, New York, 1993, 3–29).

Brian Willis, "Selling Nations: International Exhibitions and Cultural Diplomacy" (in D. Sherman and I. Rogoff, Museum Culture, Minnesota Press, Minneapolis, 1994, 265–281).

LEARNING GOALS

1. Apply the political economy of local place / global space to Bilbao.
2. Understand the strategies of place-making and how they affect our view of culture.
3. Examine the construction of place through spatial practices.
4. Assess the politics of place and identity for the global selling of a city.

WRITTEN LESSON FOR SUBMISSION

Please write a two- to three-page essay on one of the topics below.

1. Is a territorial place-based identity a good basis for progressive political mobilization or for reactionary exclusionary politics, or both? Why?
2. Has place now become more important or less important in the last 20 years? Explain.
3. How would you characterize the relationship between place and power in Bilbao?
4. Describe Bilbao's success in terms of selling place.

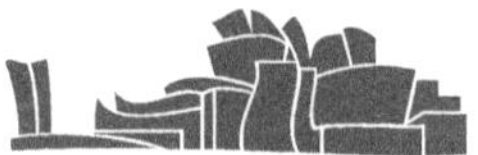

25 · Informational Bilbao

FOR DANIEL BELL, postindustrial society entails the shift from manufacturing to service economy. Science-based industries, such as computers, electronics, optics, and polymers, acquires a new centrality in such advanced societies. The shift means that society does not think of its primary product as goods, but information and knowledge. Bell observed an evolution in the nature of the productive process. The factory worker was being replaced by professional and technical jobs. Capital and labor used to form the backbone of industrial society, but now theoretical knowledge, that is, the new information and communication technologies, are becoming the principal product of the emergent postindustrial societies. The previous big shift had been from agricultural to industrial economies, but this developmental stage involves the transition from industrial to informational economies.

Not everyone agrees with this analysis. Though it is true that there are few manufacturing jobs for unskilled workers in most of the advanced capitalist societies, there is also a substantial growth in industrial manufacturing jobs across the world in countries such as China, Turkey, Brazil, India, Thailand, Malaysia, Indonesia, South Korea, and so on. Although the majority of the employment in advanced societies may be in the service sector, many of those services depend on manufacturing. Manufacturing is still a crucial element in any competitive economy. Skeptics go so far as to label the idea of a postindustrial society as a "myth," contending that what we are witnessing is the shifting from one kind of industrial economy to another. For them the service sector is manufacturing's complement, not substitute.

A new international division of labor has emerged as a consequence of the globalization of financial capital and flexible production. While automated production and skilled workers are concentrated at the center of the globalized system, low-paid and unskilled workers are scattered around the periphery. The lower cost of labor in those countries has become a magnet for multinational corporations. On the other hand, there is growth in advanced economies in low-end and unskilled occupations in the service sector accompanying the growth in professional jobs. The informational society generates an increasingly polarized social structure—the top and the bottom are expanded as the middle shrinks.

SOME ARGUE THAT this process has derived from "dependent deindustrialization" in Western nations, a phenomenon linked to the development of the Third World. The plant closures in core industrial countries and new plant openings in Third World countries are part of the same process. Transnational firms determine the future of labor and production by where they chose to invest. Total direct U.S. investment abroad was less than $50 billion in 1966; ten years later it had reached $124 billion; in another five years it surpassed $213 billion. Multinational corporations are the central economic actors in the new international order, and they have an integrated worldwide network of production, exchange, finance, and corporate services. And the role cities play in this globalized world is new and different.

The technological revolution has created globally interdependent economies. The new economic order entails a new organization of production, consumption, and circulation. In Castells's words, "It is an economy with the capacity to work as a unit in real time on a planetary scale." This does not mean that all economic processes are embraced in the global economy, but rather means that they all are affected directly or indirectly by it. In other words, the informational economy structurally determines the economic and social processes of the entire world. A worldwide network of corporations and a global network of cities are the bases for the world capitalist economy. In this respect, a new component of the present economy in the advanced Western countries is the technology park, a fashionable tool in local and regional economic development. It aims at concentrating high-technology industrial firms so that eventually enough income can be generated to sustain a region economically. High-technology products have become symbols of the informational economy. Technology parks embody the character of the new global economy. The access to theoretical knowledge (in terms of research and development) is the basis of the new productivity and competitiveness, characterized by flexible specialization.

IN 1985, BILBAO OPENED its technology park in the nearby town of Zamudio. The Basque government promoted the initiative though the Basque Regional Development Agency (SPRI), Vizcaya's Provincial Council, and the town of Zamudio. The park was designed for companies with "state-of-the-art" technology. It came equipped with important infrastructures and the most advanced technological services. Its purpose was to act as a channel for communication between research and business in order to increase the technological capacity of the entire region. In 1996, the park consisted of 64 companies employing 2,154 people. The telecommunication sector had the highest rate of investment in Zamudio, with a total of 12 enterprises and 643 employees. Their net profits that year were 39.7 billion pesetas ($250 million). A total of $55 million was invested in development and research. Approximately

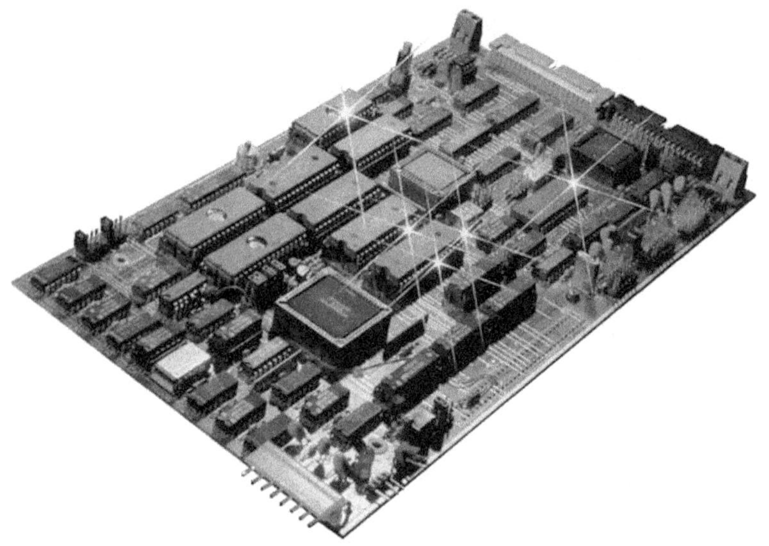

The resemblance between the architecture of a circuit board and city planning is misleading: they are shaped by different forces.

The Zamudio technology park was designed for start-ups of "state-of-the-art" companies. In fact, most of them moved in from other locations.
Photo: Getty Images Inc.

---

40 percent of the employees have a university degree and more than 20 percent are dedicated exclusively to development and research. By 1998, the number of companies had increased to 72, employing 2,300 people (28 percent of them working for research and development), and their net profits had grown to $316 million. These figures denote a substantial increase in employment in

---

Bilbao, but not necessarily a net increase in production: most of these companies were simply transferred from other locations.

CALIFORNIA'S SILICON Valley is the ideal of many deindustrialized regions. It represents the revolution in informational technologies. Its development is the outcome of the concentration of diverse elements, such as early technological innovation, its links to Stanford University, and the military industry's demand for electronic research. None of these elements play a role in Bilbao. Still, in parallel with urban renewal and architectural spectacle, a dominant discourse in the remaking of Bilbao as a significant regional city is Zamudio's technology park and the informational economy. The need to project itself as a high-tech postindustrial and financial capital in Europe's Atlantic arch, is central to Bilbao's imagemaking.

Lesson twenty-five

REQUIRED READING

Manuel Castells and Peter Hall, "Chapter 1. Technopoles: Mines and Foundries of the Informational Economy;" and "Chapter 9. Distilling the Lessons" (in M. Castells and P. Hall, Technopoles of the World. Routledge, New York, 1994).

LEARNING GOALS

1. Analyze the shift from an industrial to an information-based society.
2. Learn about the new industrial geography of postindustrial societies.
3. Assess the effects of the new economic order on cities.

4. Examine the discourse of an information-based economy in Bilbao.

WRITTEN LESSON FOR SUBMISSION

Please write a two- to three-page essay on one of the topics below.

1. What are the products and symbols of a high-tech society?
2. Explain this paradox: cities / regions appear to have less of a say these days but are very powerful when called upon to implement targeted projects in the new global economy.
3. What are the three main objectives of a technopole?
4. Is there a general formula to replicate the development of successful technology parks?
5. Discuss the presence of the informational discourse in Bilbao and its interactions (contradictions, dependencies, competitiveness, and so on) with the discourse of urban renewal.

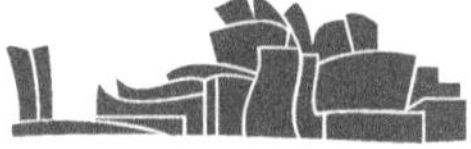

26 · The culture of tourism

THE INCREASE IN the number of tourists, and the accompanying economic benefits, help both to silence the Guggenheim critics and establish Bilbao's success story. But with tourism come side effects that greatly affect a culture. Not only are there people and objects, but there are also "traveling cultures." Travel has been essential to the commercial and industrial histories of Bilbao. The sudden influx of Guggenheim visitors (100,000 per month) is a phenomenon which intermingles tourism, economy, and culture in ways that were unknown until 1997.

Does tourism delineate a social practice? What are the distinctions among travel, tourism, leisure, hobbying, strolling, culture, pilgrimage, voyaging, excursion, and exploration? The concept of tourism encompasses several different notions. There is, for example, the basic distinction between the tourist and the traveler. The traveler only needs to arrive; the tourist needs to experience. If tourism consists of "getting away from it all," what does it mean to the quality of the tourist experience when mass tourism brings "it all" with the tourist? When the culture of tourism is more prominent than the culture the tourist is touring, is there any quality of escape left?

It is not enough to simply measure the days away from home to define a trip as tourist, nor can tourism be reduced to a set of economic activities. Questions of taste, fashion, and identity are part of the experience. Tourism and culture have always been understood to be distinct social practices, but it is better to view them as interrelated. Postmodernism denotes the conventional distinctions between high and low culture as "an economy of signs," signs that turn us into tourists and cultural consumers. Culture and street life both at home and abroad are breaking down. At the same time, Ritzer and Liska argue that tourism has become "McDisneyized," that is, people seek touristic experiences that are predictable, efficient, calculable, and controlled.

According to Rojek and Urry, tourism studies are framed around the following assumptions: "That tourism is a cultural practice; that culture and tourism hugely overlap; that tourism as a cultural practice and set of objects is highly significant or emblematic within contemporary 'Western' societies organized around mass mobility; that tourism has largely to be examined through the topics, theories and concepts of cultural analysis, especially the current foci upon issues of time and space; that there should not be a specifically *social* science of tourism; that particularly significant in the analysis of culture will be the examination of the human senses, and specially the relative importance of the sense of sight; and that none of the supposed essences of tourism, such as the notion of 'escape', provides the kind of desired conceptual unity" (*Touring Cultures*, 5.)

Some academic disciplines, such as anthropology, have had an uneasy relationship with tourism; anthropologists have always run the risk of being taken themselves for a kind of tourist. The transnational exchange during the last decades is one of tourists visiting from the north, and immigrants in search of work migrating from the south. For anthropologists, the exchange is further complicated by the fact that their former subjects from time to time come to visit them in the anthropologists' own homes.

The paradox presented by such a postmodern and postcolonial world, as argued by Graburn, is that, on the

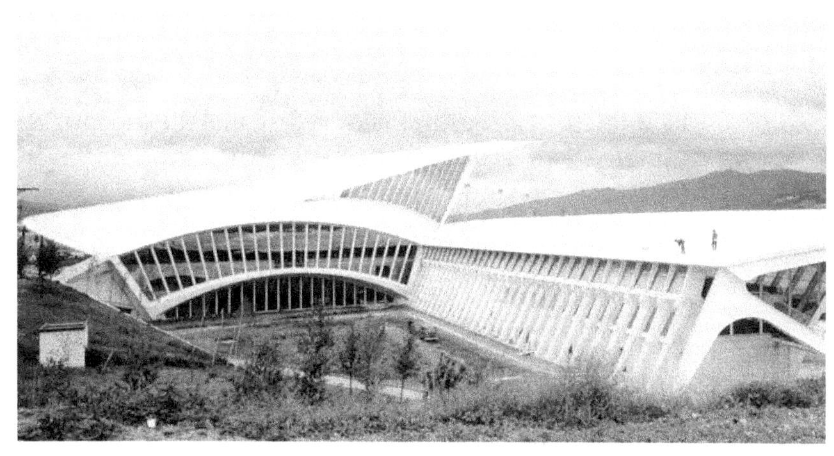

Santiago Calatrava's airport is a major component in Bilbao's ambitious 1.5 billion-dollar urban renewal plan that was put in place in the 1990s.
Photo of by José Alberto Gandía

one hand, the old metropoles are full of cultural diversity and contrasting "traditions," while on the other hand, "from a touristic point of view, the world is fast homogenizing, ... since the *same kinds* of mixtures, blends and incongruities can be found almost anywhere, channeled by the same sorts of techno-bureaucratic institutions." The superficial postmodern identities that derive from revolutions in photography and electronics, and the endless consumerism and promotion of nostalgia associated with them, raise questions about authenticity, and lead to "end of history" analyses.

ISSUES OF AUTHENTICITY point to a difference between modernist versus postmodernist tourism. Modernist tourists searched for confirmations of authentic knowledge and authentic experiences, as if authenticity should reside outside of their everyday life. To satisfy this need, the tourism industry nurtured and, where necessary, manufactured authenticity. Postmodern culture, aware of this invention of tradition and its interest in all sorts of fakery, disdains the modernist experience in favor of the "actual" experience, whatever that might be. These "cool" tourists nurture a mocking irreverence for what remains of traditional values, and have earned the sobriquet "post-tourists." "The changes of the past 25 years are so enormous," concludes Graburn, "that if the pace keeps up, in another 25 years socio-cultural differences will be further reduced and much of what travelers find in any place will already be familiar to them. Even major geographical and architectural features will be reproduced or at least familiar to most people." Bilbao, as the site of Gehry's pallid cetacean, a newly founded distinction, stands against the entropy of blurred difference. The inculcation of traditional differences in new, emblematic architecture may be the only way to preserve those differences.

CAROL BECKER'S PIECE narrates a contemporary travel experience encompassing Johannesburg, Bilbao, and New York. She assumes (quite questionably) that the Guggenheim Bilbao has nothing to do with the Basque art world: "This fabulous new building brings an international audience to Bilbao but stands apart from its cultural locality." Her article points out the enormous contradictions of a postnational aesthetics that is brought into being with conscious nationalist intentions.

Lesson twenty-six

REQUIRED READING

Jennifer Craik, "The Culture of Tourism" (in C. Rojek and J. Urry, Touring Cultures: Transformations of Travel and Theory, Routledge, New York, 1997).

Carol Becker, "The Romance of Nomadism: A Series of Reflections," (Art Journal, Summer 1999).

SUGGESTED READING

Nelson Graburn, "Tourism, Modernity and Nostalgia" (in A. Ahmed and C. Shore, The Future of Anthropology, Athlone, London, 1995).

LEARNING GOALS

1. Examine the overriding economic relevance of tourism to Bilbao.
2. Explore the cultural implications of tourism.
3. Learn about tourism and issues of authenticity, nostalgia, and postmodernism.
4. Understand the cultural and political contradictions inherent in the romance of nomadism.

WRITTEN LESSON FOR SUBMISSION

Please write a two- to three-page essay on one of the topics below.

1. Into what categories would you deconstruct the concept of tourism?
2. Describe the many ways in which culture and tourism interrelate.
3. Is cultural tourism as lofty as its advocates would have us believe?
4. What does the distinction between "modern" and "postmodern" tourism add to your understanding of the present culture of Bilbao?
5. Do you agree or disagree with Becker's assumption that the Bilbao Guggenheim stands apart from its cultural locality? Explain.

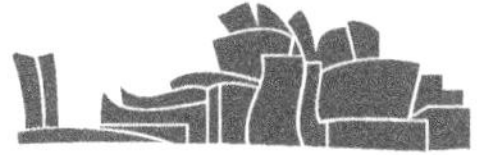

27 · Reinvention and millennialism

Thinking the futures

BILBAO ONCE HAD little choice but to view history as a discourse of ruin. Throughout the 1990s Bilbao was compelled to think of the future in the millennial terms of brand new beginnings and daring reinventions. Only "Bilbao 2000" mattered.

Only a century and a half-ago, preindustrial Bilbao was a small provincial town of 18,000 merchants and artisans surrounded by rural life. At the turn of the last century European multinationals and the local mining landlords turned the Nervión's left bank's mountain of iron into a hot commodity. Imperial Great Britain imported two-thirds of her iron from Bilbao. The mining boom was over by the beginning of this century, but the iron and steel industries, led by Altos Hornos de Vizcaya, endured alternate periods of prosperity and crisis until the 1990s. Spain's entry into the newly configured European Union forced Bilbao's antiquated metallurgical complex to shut down. The city's unemployment rate throughout the 1990s has been about 25 percent (as high as 60 percent for the youth). Heavy industry is gone, but its legacy of polluted rivers, contaminated soils, and urban ruin (a museum of ecological horrors) will remain for a long time. In the last two decades Bilbao's population has decreased almost 20 percent, from about 430,000 to 360,000.

Were it not for the spectacular visual force of her ruins, and now her emblematic buildings, the Guggenheim, the metro, *Euskalduna*, and others, Bilbao would be a typical European provincial city exuding bourgeois lifestyle. If in the past it was the aesthetics of the "tough city" that set Bilbao apart (see chapter nineteen), one must now add the aesthetics of the "soft city"—the city of illusion, seduction, myth, and spectacular architecture.

BILBAO'S DEMOGRAPHIC decline, postindustrial ruin, and ecological devastation would make one wonder whether 1990 Bilbao had any future at all, let alone the luxury of dreaming of millennial rebirth. It is not nostalgic lament for a ruined city that one hears in Bilbao. One is struck by the high expectations of a city that aspires to become, once again, its region's main industrial and commercial port, "the *cabecera* [masthead] of the Atlantic Arch stretching from Santiago de Compostela to Bordeaux," as touted in promotional literature. Bilbao hopes to be the main informational and touristic city of the Basque region, and even, in partnership with New York, one of the European capitals of art, museums, and elite tourism. A postmodern sensibility attuned to the catastrophes of this apocalyptic century, backed by a willingness to learn from the ruins of history, might fall under the panoramic spell of Bilbao's industrial wasteland and ecological horror. But such appreciation doesn't encompass the "museum" motif Bilbao planners envision to attract the mass tourism they hope will provide economic revitalization.

If ruins call for new architecture and new millennial beginnings, Bilbao seems ready to produce them aplenty. As we know from previous chapters, the demise of former industries on the left bank's riverfront leaves large parcels of land close to the city well-suited for major redevelopment projects. The ambitious redevelopment plan includes Foster's metro, Calatrava's airport and bridge, Sterling / Wilford's transport hub project, Soriano / Palacio's *Euskalduna* Convention Center and Music Hall, and Gehry's Guggenheim, as well as the new one-million-square-foot office and shopping mall complex

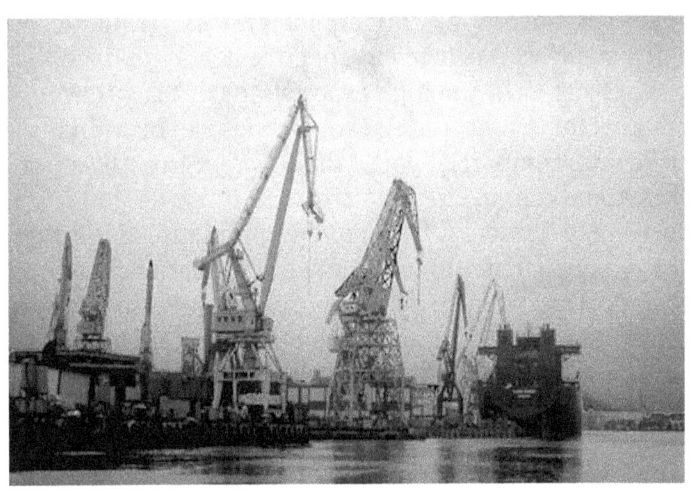

The left bank, before the change. "The Nervión valley, smoking with a hundred chimneys, forms a spectacle that is so stunning as to become unforgettable," wrote Max Weber in 1897.
Photo: Iñaki Uriarte.

---

development on the Abandoibarra riverfront by Cesar Pelli.

As everyone knows by now, Gehry's volcano of a building occupies center stage in Bilbao's newly crafted image. It has overshadowed all the other projects by drawing the necessary international attention to put Bilbao "on the map." The architecture is fiery, as befits

---

Bilbao's plethora of dialectical images. A titanium cetacean, the only white building in her streets: perhaps it's a moon fallen from New York. In any case, it is the shining emblem of Bilbao's new beauty. It was not Brecht but Benjamin who became obsessed with the Parisian Arcades and the lost aura of art and modernity (see next chapter) would be intoxicated by the architectural spectacle amid the rubble of the "tough city." Conceived and built to serve global imagery and mass tourism, this is no Brechtian socialist utopia, but rather the quintessential architectural expression of an ambitious nationalist Basque program.

Bilbao's millennialism raises the question of the possibilities for utopian thought in contemporary culture. Levitas concludes that such thinking is difficult but necessary. In most classical leftist thinking, "utopia implies drawing up blueprints for the future and supposing that they can be realized through sheer force of will." Anti-utopian arguments, on the other hand, "identify utopia with blueprints of future societies which inevitably, if attempts are made to realize them, lead to totalitarianism." One task of critical thinking is to help insure that Bilbao's heavy emphasis on the future, often at the expense of the present, not be allowed to foster totalitarian social structures.

THE DIFFICULTY DOES not lie in conjuring up fancy futures; Bilbao has proven it can dream. The difficulty lies rather in adequately mapping the present to establish meaningful connections with and allow for real transformations into the imagined future. Otherwise dreams for the future will not prove to have been utopian, but just stale mythologies, a propaganda ploy for the dominant ideology of urban renewal and salvation by architecture. Ernst Bloch's distinctions between abstract and concrete utopias, between expressions of wishful thinking, compensatory desire, escapist ideology, versus expressions real hope and actual transformative action, are as pertinent as ever.

Many modernist thinkers claimed that art was the bearer of futuristic and utopian thinking. Architecture in Bilbao has taken on that mantle. For Adorno art is "a recollection of the possible with a critical edge against the real; it is a kind of imaginary restitution of that catastrophe which is world history." For Marcuse, "Art cannot change the world, but it can contribute to changing the consciousness and drives of men and women who could change the world." The agency of transformation, then, is no longer the working class, but art. Still, if revolutionary art was the avant garde of the Great Refusal, Bilbao's spectacular architecture—the beneficiary of disproportionate subsidies from the public funds for culture—is anything but refusal of the status quo. Architecture has become the dominant urban ideology, displacing all other alternative futures. Hailed as a beacon to attract international fame and generate a touristic economy, it has overshadowed the need to identify other cultural and political agencies for social transformation.

Lesson twenty-seven

REQUIRED READING

Ruth Levitas, "The Future of Thinking About the Future" and Dick Hebdige, "Training Some Thoughts on the Future" (in Jon Bird, et al., Mapping the Futures: Local Cultures, Global Change. Routledge, London, 1993, 257–266 and 270–279).

LEARNING GOALS

1. Assess the ideological role of the concept of "future" in Bilbao's urban renewal projects.
2. Define millennialism.
3. Understand the relevance of spectacular architecture in futuristic discourse.
4. Evaluate the role of utopian thinking in Bilbao's transformation and why it has become increasingly difficult to believe in utopian transformations.

WRITTEN LESSON FOR SUBMISSION

Please write a two- to three-page essay on one of the topics below.

1. Should "the future" become a central ideological tenet in the urban renewal process? Explain.
2. How do discourses about the future turn into mythologies?
3. Assess the need for and problems with utopian thinking in contemporary postmodern culture.
4. Is there a lag of agencies for social transformation in Bilbao? Explain.
5. How would you square Bilbao's millennialism with Raymond Williams's premise that "culture is ordinary"?

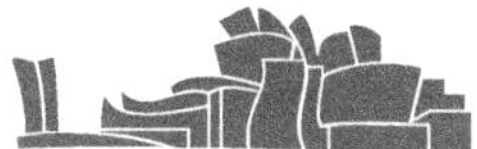

28 · Bilbao: ruin, architecture, and allegory

One wonders what sort of allegory (poetic, historical, or political) Bertolt Brecht hoped to evoke when he wrote, "How beautiful, how beautiful, how beautiful is the moon of Bilbao, the most beautiful city of the continent." It may have been a clear moon rising irresistibly from Somorrostro's hills over the nocturnal golden glare of the Nervión River's left bank, its glow of molten metal from distant blast furnaces suffusing the sky. Or was it perhaps the Dantean spectacle of a twelve-mile long string of artificial iron and steel volcanoes interspersed among the green hills, valleys and rivers of a lush territory extolled by travelers as a paradise? Or might it have been the dream of a revolutionary utopia rising from socialist Bilbao that compelled him to marvel at Bilbao's dark beauty? A writer as prophetic as Brecht surely was aware of the dialectics of the metallic fiery sun of Pliny's "mountain of iron" and the quietly imperious moon extending her redeeming mantle of silent, pure light over the shadowy people, waters, and valleys below.

"Nothing in the world is more magnificent than these mines," Max Weber had written earlier in 1897, while noting the workers' "sometimes repellent filth." The letter to his mother Helene Weber continued: "The panorama of the mountains ... rising up above the sea and the Nervión valley, smoking with a hundred chimneys, forms a spectacle that is simply so stunning as to become unforgettable." At the conclusion of the letter he regrets having to leave Las Arenas, on the right bank of the Nervión, "because the beach here is marvelous, the waves have gigantic force and the entire area is beautiful."

It is over this smoldering valley with chimneys exuding clouds of smoke, mountains stripped naked by the sea, and beaches and rocks lashed by waves that Brecht must have, in his imagination, seen his beautiful moon rising. It still rises, but the foundries are stilled, their chimneys felled by the dynamite of squads of demolition workers. There are no manufactured volcanoes left to illumine the night. Brecht might say that the lunar light now longs for redemption of the missing fire, blood and sweat that was Bilbao in the last century. All that remains of the famed, now extinguished blast furnaces is a wasteland of cold ruins waiting to be reproduced in some more peripheral area, as suits the capitalist motif of the moment.

BRECHT'S CLOSE FRIEND Walter Benjamin would surely have been fascinated by the new Bilbao and in particular by the spectacular success of the Bilbao Guggenheim Museum. Bilbao, with its vast landscape of ruins, would first evoke to Benjamin the catastrophe of history spread out before Paul Klee's *Angelus Novus* with wings spread, eyes wide open staring into relentless waves of wreckage heaped upon wreckage, the "storm from Paradise" impelling him into the future with his back turned, "while the pile of debris before him grows towards the sky." In a Vizcayan sky full of smoke and debris, Bilbao's present postindustrial landscape, with ashes grown cold and only a burning memory of fire, would have rekindled Benjamin's impression of history as decay and ruin. But even Benjamin might come to the realization that the glare of calderous volcanic fires has not departed the skies of Bilbao, but has been transfigured. Indeed, there could be no more volcanic building, a spectacle of bright bursting yellows, whites, and oranges glowingly exclaiming, "Miracles still occur." Out of this space between ruins and miracles, past and present, sky and ground, intense with mournful loss and awakened allegory, arises something distinctly Bilbaoan which may offer a hint of lost aura. We must traverse that space to understand the Bilbao *fin de millennium*.

Bilbao is a city beset by powerful antinomies emerging from contrasting traditions, whose uneasy encounter with the mythified globalism of a new millennial future presents varying kinds of resistance. What sort of historical plot to embrace: romantic, tragic, ironic, or pastiche? What kind of symbolism to experience: mythic, allegorical, utopian, or redemptive? What kind of time frame to invoke: past foundations, present transience, or future rebirth? Also at issue is what kind of basic political and cultural legitimacies to promote: Spanish, Basque, European, or global? These central antinomian realities enrich and afflict Bilbao on the millennial edge. They provide unique opportunities for a city compelled to confront her ruins and reinvent herself. It is crucial that the existence of the antinomies be recognized and their nature explored. This critical task demands that the dialectical tension between the symbolism of allegory (the staggering industrial ruins, the obsolescence of outdated ideologies, the suffering of unemployed and marginal groups), and the symbolism of myth (the brilliance of Gehry's building, the millennial discourses of future globalization, and the passionate vision of city planners) be investigated and celebrated.

THIS SMOKELESS "blast furnace" for an informational economy, internationally celebrated, its image mechanically reproduced and widely disseminated, would draw Benjamin's attention irresistibly. The museum is an urban phantasmagoria by means of which a culture is being reproduced, reinvented, and reinvigorated. It tells the story of the rise of new

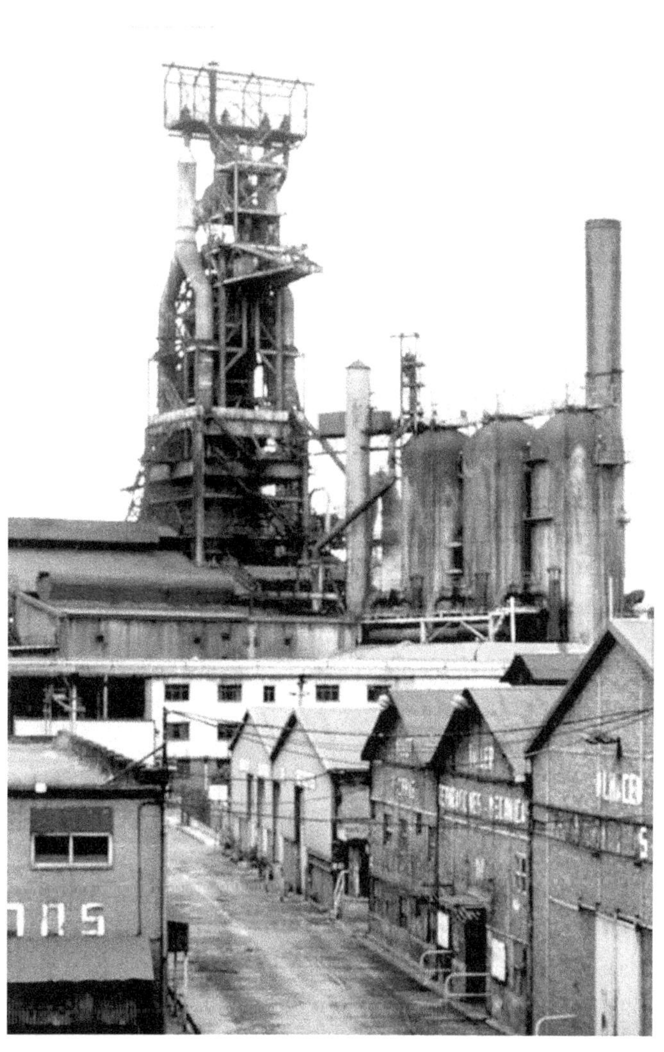

One of the blast furnaces or Altos Hornos, monuments to the rustbelt and the visionaries who created them. Bilbao must search out her most cherished truths, her tough beauty, from the debris of her own history. *Photo: Iñaki Uriarte.*

urban regeneration in which architectural spectacle and ideology are put directly in the service of economics: a monument created to woo tourists. Haussmann's state-financed, wholesale "strategic beautification" of Paris is the most obvious antecedent, and Leiris's comparison between museums and brothels leaps to mind. For dialectical thought willing to consider the positive and negative poles of historical processes—the rubbish of outdated buildings and cultures and the unprecedented material destruction of ruined industries, in contrast with the liberating potential of the new technologies and fetishistic images—Bilbao's postindustrial experiment is fascinating.

AT THE SAME TIME Bilbao's new aura and fetishism, her new *distance*, is bound up with a globalization controlled financially and artistically from the United States. The mythology of the past is unabashedly commandeered to serve the mythology of the future. But it is at this juncture that the antinomian reality of cultural creation must be kept alive.

It was the destiny of Gehry's Guggenheim to become the emblem of Bilbao's reinvention. The consequences of such mythification will depend on how the allegorical nature of the building ties into Bilbao's physical and social ruins. Will the building stand in dialectical opposition to the rusty, silent, imposing, dramatic, empty Altos Hornos blast furnaces of Sestao, just a few miles down the riverfront, turning Gehry's masterpiece into the architectural equivalent of a Dantean song? Or, once the closed blast furnaces are demolished, obliterating once and for all the industrial allegories of transitory progress and unemployment, will the museum be perceived as merely the founding edifice of a Bilbao-scale Haussmannian urban transformation? The emblem can also turn into a dialectically constructed historical object. The ideological seduction may give birth to a politically charged discontinuity with history's various myths of progress. In short, will the myth also become a critical allegory of its own foundations? Or will it be merely an accomplice to the "Benetton effect," art co-opted by the commodified and promotional culture of department stores, tourism agencies, city planners, and nationalist politicians?

Certain historical periods foster allegorical experience, recovering otherwise irretrievably lost cultural treasures. The potential rewards of an allegorical reading of Bilbao's buildings, social groups, and cultural traditions are enormous. For Bilbao is also the faces of the unemployed, of early-retired workers, uprooted migrants and prostitutes, marginalized youths and artists, jailed draft dodgers, and cloistered nuns. Bilbao can only be understood through a dialectics of seeing, past the veil of its industrial ruins and ideological constructs.

ALLEGORY CAN TRANSCEND beauty. Allegory can glory in transience, ripeness, and decay. The miraculous beauty and transfigured reality brought into existence by the Bilbao Guggenheim may in the end prove only to be sleight of hand, aesthetic imposture indifferent to its historical and social context. The allegory of decaying bodies and structures does not falsify transience and suffering. The positive bias of spectacular architecture, the totalistic pretense of incarnate, fixed beauty, stands against the allegorical fragments of the brevity and instability of blast furnace ruins. Bilbao must preserve the critical force of allegory, beyond beauty, to recover aesthetically what has been lost historically. Otherwise, Bilbao's hard urban aesthetics, which have proven capable of integrating debris, landscape, ugliness, migration, and resistance, and which awed Bertolt Brecht and Max Weber, Oteiza, Serra, and Gehry will be supplanted by the harmonious pretensions of beauty orchestrated for the touristic voyeurism of visitors and locals alike. This critical force demands a willingness to search out Bilbao's most cherished truths, her tough beauty, from within the garbage heap of her history.

Lesson twenty-eight

REQUIRED READING

Walter Benjamin, "Paris, Capital of the Nineteenth Century" (Exposé of 1939) (in W. Benjamin, The Arcades Project, Harvard Univ. Press, Cambridge, 1999).

SUGGESTED READING

Susan Buck-Morss, "Mythic History: Fetish" (S. Buck Morss, The Dialectics of Seeing: Walter Benjamin and the Arcades Project, M.I.T. Press, Cambridge, 1989).

LEARNING GOALS

1. Apply Benjamin's perspective on the nineteenth-century urban phantasmagoria of Paris to Bilbao.
2. Assess "newness" and "antiquity" in the renewal projects of a postindustrial city such as Bilbao from a dialectical viewpoint.
3. Examine the historical role of modern architecture in relation to engineering, technology, photography, film, and the media.
4. Critically frame the historical tension between myth and allegory in the urban political realities of Bilbao.

WRITTEN LESSON FOR SUBMISSION

Please write a two- to three-page essay on one of the topics below.

---

1. Comment on Baudelaire's dictum, "Everything for me becomes allegory."
2. How can the central historical tensions between myth and allegory and between conformity and criticism be resolved in Bilbao?
3. What do you make of the Weber / Brecht / Benjamin associations with Bilbao?
4. Discuss the arguments for and against the proposition that architecture for Bilbao will be the pro-genitor of utopia.
5. Discuss the various dialectics and antinomies at work in Bilbao. What sort of Bilbao do you think will have emerged by the time Gehry's Guggenheim becomes an accepted and integrated fixture in the city's life?

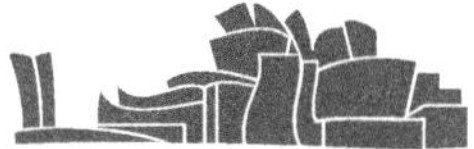

Pictures

Jost Amman woodcuts. *Kunstbuchlein* (1599.) 89, 172.
Ibon Aranberri. Photographs of Bilbao Guggenheim. Cover, 8, 118.
Barbie® doll shown courtesy of Mattel, Inc. ©2002 Mattel, Inc. All rights reserved. 172.
School of Thomas Bewick. *Engravings*. 18.
Bilbao map. By kind permission of Bilbao central archives 32.
Seymour Chwast illustrations. Copyright ©1995 Flat File Editions Inc. 95, 150.
José Alberto Gandía. Photograph of the Arriaga Theater main facade. 38. Zubizuri bridge. 98. Bilbao airport 184.
FOAT aerial photography. Abandoibarra riverfront development. 83.
Motherboard photograph. Copyright ©2002 Getty Images Inc. 179.
Paul Klee: Angelus Novus (1920.) By permission of the estate of Paul Klee. Israel Museum, Jerusalem, 62.
Jorge Oteiza sculptures. By permission of the artist. 134, 139.
ES & Robinson's, manufacturer of paper bags. Sample book engraving. 26.
Oliviero Toscani photograph. Courtesy of the Benetton Group. 159.
Unknown photographer: Lotte Lenya. Kurt Weill Foundation for Music, New York. 48.
Iñaki Uriarte. Photographs. 124, 189, 196. Altos Hornos, 196.

Select Bibliography

by Nancy Faires

Audiovisuals

Artful Architecture: The Getty Center and the Guggenheim Museum Bilbao. Elizabeth Farnsworth, Jeffrey Kaye, and Jim Lehrer. Films for the Humanities and Sciences, 1999.

Charlie Rose: Frank Gehry, Terrence McNally and Joe Mantello (Show #1902). Rose Communications, Inc., WNET, 800 All News, Inc., 1997.

Frank Gehry Uncensored. Dir. of photography Scott Barnett. Host Jana Wendt. Films for the Humanities and Sciences, 1999.

Guggenheim Museum Bilbao. Dir. David Collier. Prod. Adeline Collier. Narrator Sam West. Films for the Humanities and Sciences, 1999.

Guggenheim Museum, Bilbao. Dir. David Collier. Prod. Adeline Collier. Narrator Sam West. Insite Video Communications, 1999.

Guggenheim Museum, Bilbao. Dir. Gary Deans. Prod. Alan Hall, Jana Wendt. ABC, 1998.

Guggenheim Museum, Bilbao. Frank O. Gehry. Slide progam. Guggenheim, 1998.

Guggenheim Museum: Bilbao Exterior Views. Slide program. Harthill Art Associates, 1999.

Guggenheim Museum: Bilbao Interior Views. Slide program. Harthill Art Associates, 1999.

Revolution in a Box. Host Forrest Sawyer. ABC News Nightline, 1997.

Vieja luna de Bilbao. Prod. Hegaz TV and Film. Euskal Telebista, 2001.

Books

Asensio Cerver, Francisco. *The Architecture of Museums*. Trans. Mark Lodge. New York: Hearst Books, 1997.

Blistène, Bernard and Lisa Dennison, curators. *Rendezvous: Masterpieces from the Centre Georges Pompidou and the*

———. *Guggenheim Museums*. New York / Paris: H. N. Abrams, 1998.

Bechtler, Christina, ed. *Frank O. Gehry, Kurt W. Forster*. Ostfildern-Ruit, Germany: Cantz, 1999.

Bruggen, Coosje van. *Frank O. Gehry: Guggenheim Museum Bilbao*. New York: Guggenheim Museum Publications, 1997.

Bruggen, Coosje van. *Frank O. Gehry: Guggenheim Museum Bilbao*. New York: H. N. Abrams, 1998.

Cohen, Jean-Louis, et al. *Frank Gehry, Architect*. New York: Harry N. Abrams, 2001.

Dal Co, Francesco and Kurt W. Forster. *Frank O. Gehry: The Complete Works*. New York: Monacelli, 1998.

Donzel, Catherine. *New Museums*. Paris: Telluri, 1998.

Esteban Azurmendi, Iñaki, José Antonio González Carrera, and Alberto Tellitu Apiolea. *El milagro Guggenheim: Una ilusión de alto riesgo*. Basque Country, Spain: Diario El Correo, S. A.: 1997.

Forster, Kurt Walter. *Frank O. Gehry: Guggenheim Bilbao Museoa*. London / Stuttgart: Edition Axel Menges, 1998.

Friedman, Mildred S., ed. *Gehry Talks: Architecture + Process*. New York: Rizzoli, 1999.

G.A. document 54, Guggenheim Bilbao Museoa, Frank O. Gehry. Tokyo: A. D. A. Edita, 1998.

Gehry, Frank O. *Guggenheim Bilbao Museoa*. London: Edition Axel Menges, 1998.

Guggenheim Bildumaren Maisu-Lan Modernoak. Bilbao: Solomon R. Guggenehim, 1994.

Henderson, Justin. *Museum Architecture*. Gloucester, Massachusetts: Rockport Publishers, 1998.

Jodidio, Philip. *Frank O. Gehry*. New York: Taschen, 1998.

Museo Guggenheim Bilbao: estudio de viabilidad. Bilbao: Diputación Foral de Bizkaia, 1992.

Museo Guggenheim Bilbao: plan operativo a cuatro años. Bilbao: Solomon R. Guggenheim Foundation Museum, 1995.

Newhouse, Victoria. "The Guggenheim Museum, Bilbao." *Towards a New Museum*. New York: Monacelli Press, 1998. 245–59.

Rolin, Jean. *Bilbao, le musée Guggenheim de Frank Gehry: Brasilia 1957–1997*. Paris: L'Architecture d'aujourd'hui, 1997.

Romoli, Giorgio. *Frank O. Gehry: Museo Guggenheim, Bilbao*. Torino: Testo and Immagine, 1999.

Ros, Xon de. "The Guggenheim Museum Bilbao: High Art as Popular Culture." *Constructing Identity in Contemporary Spain: Theoretical Debates and Cultural Practice*. Ed. Jo Labanyi. Oxford: Oxford University Press, 2002. 280–93.

Stoller, Ezra. *Guggenheim New York and Guggenheim Bilbao*. New York: Princeton Architectural Press, 1999.

Suau, John Thomas. "The Guggenheim Museum Bilbao: Cultural Tourism, Urban Renewal, and Political Risk." Master of Arts Thesis. American University, 1999.

Svenson, Hope. "Gehry's Guggenheim Bilbao: The Art Museum Re-defined." Div. III Exam. Hampshire College, 1999.

Zulaika, Joseba. *Crónica de una seducción: El Museo Guggenheim Bilbao*. Madrid: Nerea, 1997.

———. " 'Miracle in Bilbao': Basques in the Casino of Globalism." *Basque Cultural Studies*. Ed. William A. Douglass, Carmelo Urza, Linda White, and Joseba Zulaika. Reno: Basque Studies Program UNR, 1999. 262–74.

———. "Tough Beauty." *Iberian Cities*. Ed. Joan Ramon Resina. New York and London, Routledge, 2001. 1–17.

Journals

Andrews, Suzanna. "Self-Confidence Man." *New York* 9 May 1994: 44–53.

Attias, Laurie. "Art of This Century: Guggenheim Museum Bilbao." *ARTnews* Dec. 1997: 184.

———. "C'mon Let's Twist Again." *ARTnews* Oct. 1996: 124–26.

———. "The Guggenheim Bilbao." *ARTnews* Sept. 1997: 144.

Barreneche, Raul A. "Gehry's Guggenheim." *Architecture* Sept. 1996: 177–81.

Baxter, Joell. "Guggenheim Proposes New Gehry Museum." *New Art Examiner* Dec. / Jan. 1999 / 2000: 14.

———

Becker, Carol. "The Romance of Nomadism: A Series of Reflections." *Art Journal* Summer 1999: 22–29.

Béret, Chantal. "Bilbao Effects." *Art Press* Jan. 2000: 92.

"Bomb in Bilbao." *Flash Art* Nov. / Dec. 1997: 56.

Bradley, Kim. "The Deal of the Century." *Art in America* July 1997: 48–55, 105–06.

———. "Guggenheim Bilbao Taking Shape." *Art in America* Feb. 1995: 27.

Brandolini, Sebastiano. "The Guggenheim Museum in Bilbao." *Domus* Nov. 1997: 10–19.

Buren, Daniel. "C'est pour moi la Tour Eiffel des musées." *Connaissance des Arts* 545 (1997): 47–48.

Came, Barry. "Spain's New Wonder of the World." *McLean's*. 3 Nov. 1997: 62–64.

Campbell, Clayton, Helena Kontova, and Giancarlo Politi. "Frank Gehry: The Artist Is the Pig, The Architect Is the Chicken." *Flash Art* Jan. / Feb. 1998: 76–81.

Cembalest, Robin. "Art Note: Controversial Bid to Show Picasso's *Guernica* at Guggenheim Museum Bilbao, Spain." *New Art Examiner* July–Aug. 1997: 58.

———. "Bilbao Opens: Terrorists Foiled." *ARTnews* Dec. 1997: 66.

———. "First We Take Bilbao." *ARTnews* Sept. 1997: 63–64.

———. "The Guggenheim's High-Stakes Gamble." *ARTnews* May 1992: 84–92.

———. "Then We Take Berlin." *ARTnews* Sept. 1997: 64.

Cibulski, Dana Mouton. "Basque-ing in the Glory." *Art Papers* Nov. / Dec. 1999: 16.

Cohn, David. "Big Business in Bilbao." *World Architecture* Dec.1997–Jan. 1998: 60–61.

Cramer, Ned. "Guggenheim Stokes Basque Economy." *Architecture* Feb. 1999: 31.

Dannatt, Adrian. "Architecture Versus Image." *Building Design* 23 May 1997: 6.

D'Arcy, David. "A Dream of Ships and Steel: The Guggenheim Museum Bilbao. Interview with Frank Gehry, Architect." *The Art Newspaper* Oct. 1997: 14.

D'Arcy, David. "No Populist, No Colonialist—Just Loved by Business. Interview with Thomas Krens." *The Art Newspaper* Oct. 1998: 36–37.

D'Souza, Aruna. "Sculpture in the Space of Architecture." *Art in America* Feb. 2000: 84–89.

Decker, Andrew. "Can the Guggenheim Pay the Price?" *ARTnews* Jan. 1994: 142–49.

———. "What Price Guggenheim?" *Village Voice* 23 June 1992: 39–42.

Dysart, Dinah. "Guggenheim Bilbao: Art and Architecture Find a Perfect Match." *Art and Australia* 36 (1999): 342–43.

Eakin, Hugh and Veronica Goyzueta. "From Bilbao to Brazil?" *ARTnews* Jan. 2000: 49.

Esterow, Milton. "How Do You Top This?" *ARTnews* Summer 1998: 74–76.

Failing, Patricia. "Judd and Panza Square Off." *ARTnews* Nov. 1990: 146–51.

Filler, Martin. "Ghosts in the House: The Role of the Architect as Artist." *New York Review of Books* 21 Oct. 1999: 10+.

Gargiani, Roberto. "Frank O. Gehry: Guggenheim Museum Bilbao, Spain." *Casabella* 60 (1996): 2–15.

Garza Carvajal, Federico. "The Guggenheim Museum, Bilbao: A Titanium Whale Sets Anchor on the Nervion River." *Art Nexus* May / July 1998: 68–70.

"The Getty Center / Guggenheim Museum Bilbao." *Architecture* Dec. 1997: 55.

Giovannini, Joseph. "Gehry's Reign in Spain." *Architecture* Dec. 1997: 64–77.

———. "Getty v. Guggenheim: A Paradigm Apart." *Art in America* July 1998: 80–85.

———. "Reshaping Bilbao." *Architecture* Dec. 1997: 39–42.

Goldberger, Paul. "The Politics of Building: For the Basques, the Guggenheim Museum Bilbao Is a Declaration of Their Presence in the World." *The New Yorker* 13 Oct. 1997: 48–49, 53.

Gough, Piers. "The Building As Jujitsu: Career of Frank O. Gehry and the New Guggenheim Museum Bilbao, Spain." *Modern Painters* 9 (1996): 50–55.

———

"Guggenheim Gets Going with Plea for *Guernica*." *Art Newspaper* July / Aug. 1996: 13.

"Guggenheim Museum Bilbao, Spain." *Lotus International* 85 (1995): 64–73.

"Guggenheim Museum Bilbao." *Abitare* Oct. 1997: 69–70, 72.

Guilbaut, Serge. "Recycling or Globalizing the Museum: MOMA-Guggenheim Approaches." *Parachute* Oct. / Dec. 1998: 63–67.

Hill, Albert. "It Ain't What You Do ... Andy Warhol: A Factory." *Blueprint* Jan. 2000: 80.

Irace, Fulvio. "Due città per due musei: Frank O. Gehry's Guggenheim Museum in Bilbao and Richard Meier's Getty Center in Los Angeles Seen in Relation to Their Cities." *Abitare* March 1998: 123–25.

Ivy, Robert. "Frank Gehry: Plain Talk with a Master." *Architectural Record* May 1999: 185–92, 356, 359, 360.

Jodidio, Philip. "Le musée nouveau de Bilbao à Londres." *Connaissance des Arts* March 1999: 5.

———. "Un nouvel imperialisme?" *Connaissance des Arts* Dec. 1997: 7.

Johnson, Ken. "Starship Guggenheim." *Art in America* Sept. 1992: 106–19.

Kaufman, Jason Edward. "Maker of World-Class Art Museums." *Art Newspaper* Oct. 1997: 15.

Kramer, Hilton. "The New Guggenheim 'Galaxy': Dispersing a Museum Collection." *New Criterion* Sept. 1992: 4–9.

Kubany, Elizabeth Harrison and Suzanne Stephens. "Small Museums: The Ant-Bilbao." *Architectural Record* Jan. 2000: 113–32.

Landi, Ann. "The 50 Most Powerful People in the Art World." *ARTnews* n.n. 1995: 52.

Larrauri, Eva. "Beyond the Guggenheim." *ARTnews* April 1999: 95.

Larson, Soren. "A Star is Born." *Architectural Record* March 2000: 29.

Lewis, Michael J. "The Guggenheim in Bilbao." *New Criterion* Oct. 1997: 52–54.

Lind, Maria. "Cumulus: Aus Europa." *Parkett* 53 (1998): 186–91.
Lister, David. "Built for Art." *Modern Painters* 10 (1997): 68–69.
Lyall, Sutherland. "Building Favourites." *The Architect's Journal* 208 (1998): 13.
MacClancy, Jeremy. "The Museum As a Site of Contest: The Bilbao Guggenheim." *Focaal* 29 (1997): 91–100.
Mantegna, Gianfranco. "Report From Spain: A Museum for the 21st Century—Frank Gehry's Bilbao Guggenheim." *Graphis* 313 (1998): 110.
Martínez, Rosa. "Guggenheim Bilbao: What Lies Behind the Titanium Splendor?" *Flash Art* Jan. / Feb. 1998: 81–84.
"A 'Miracle' of the 'Times': Herbert Muschamp's Reviews of Frank Gehry." *New Criterion* Oct. 1997: 1–3.
Mitchell, William J. "A Tale of Two Cities: Architecture and the Digital Revolution." *Science* 6 August 1999: 839, 841.
"Museums Galore." *Economist* 19 Feb. 2000: 82–85.
Nicolin, Pierluigi. "The Dismemberment of Orpheus." *Lotus International* 98 (1998): 6–26.
Pacheco, Patrick. "Bilbao Battles for *Guernica*." *Art and Antiques* Oct. 1997: 19.
Papay, Kate. "The Guggenheim Tries to Grow." *ARTnews* Nov. 1999: 66.
Pawley, Martin. "Lessons Learned from a Tale of Two Galleries." *The Architect's Journal* 29 April 1999: 18.
Pissarro, Joachim. "Gehry's Guggenheim Museum in Bilbao." *Apollo* Dec. 1997: 51–52.
Prud Homme, Alex. "The CEO of Culture Inc." *Time* 20 Jan. 1992: 36.
Rainbird, Sean. "Bilbao Guggenheim Museum." *Burlington Magazine* Jan. 1998: 62–64.
Raine, Craig. "Gehry's Supreme Fiction." *Modern Painters* Winter 1998: 32–35.
Rambert, Francis. "Bilbao: Sous le signe de mouvement." *Connaissance des Arts* 544 (1997): 32–33.
Raphel, Murray. "A Guided Tour of the Bilbao Guggenheim with Murray Raphel." *Art Business News* Sept. 1999: 72.

Raphel, Murray. "One on One with the Director." *Art Business News* Sept. 1999: 72.

Richardson, John. "Go Go Guggenheim." *The New York Review of Books* 16 July 1992: 18–22.

Richter, Ralph. "Frank O. Gehry: Guggenheim Museum Bilbao, Spain." *Architecture and Urbanism* July 1998: 110–29.

Romoli, Giorgio. "Gehry in Bilbao: A Different Interpretation." *L'Architettura* Feb. 1998: 121–23.

Rosenthal, Tom. "Kentucky Fried Guggenheim." *Art Review* June 1998: 54–55.

Rossi, Sara. "I miracoli della grande architettura moderna." *L'Architettura* Apr. 1999: 263.

"Spanish Guggenheim on Target: Bilbao." *Art Newspaper* Nov. 1994: 17.

Stein, Karen D. "Project Diary: Frank Gehry's Dream Project, The Guggenheim Museum Bilbao, Draws the World to Spain's Basque Country." *Architectural Record* Oct. 1997: 74–87.

Stephens, Suzanne. "The Bilbao Effect." *Architectural Record* May 1999: 168–73.

Stolz, George. "Bilbao to Bid for *Guernica*." *ARTnews* Jan. 1997: 47.

———. "Spain: Taking the Art out of Politics." *ARTnews* Feb. 1995: 108.

Stungo, Naomi. "Shine. Building Preview: Guggenheim Museum Bilbao, Spain." *RIBA* June 1997: 20–21.

Sullivan, Ann C. "Gehry's Guggenheim on Display in Venice." *Architecture* Aug. 1995: 27.

Thea, Carolee. "The Guggenheim Museum in Bilbao." *Sculpture* Feb. 1998: 71–73.

"Thomas Krens: Guggenheim nouvelle donne." *Connaissance des Arts* March 1999: 106–07.

Tomkins, Calvin. "The Maverick: Why Is Frank Gehry a Genius Everywhere But in His Own Home Town?" *The New Yorker* 7 July 1997: 38–45.

Von der Becke, Alex. "A Futurist Triumph for Spain." *Museums Journal* 98 (1998): 25.

Webb, Michael. "Realizing Frank O. Gehry's Vision and Challenging Contemporary Artists." *Architecture and Urbanism* July 1998: 130–37.

Weideger, Paula. "The Supreme Commander of the Guggenheim Empire: Guggenheim Foundation Director Thomas Krens." *New Statesman* 20 Feb. 1998: 42.

Wiebrecht, Ulrike. "The Guggenheim Effect." *Der Baumeister* Oct. 1999: 26–31.

Zorpette, Glenn. "Star Search." *ARTnews* Nov. 1991: 126–29.

Zuck, Barbara. "Gaga Over Guggenheim." *Columbus Dispatch* 31 May 1998, Features: 1J.

Zulaika, Joseba. "On the Seduction of Architectural Miracles." *Neon* Summer 1998.

———. "Postindustrial Bilbao: The Reinvention of a New City." *Basque Studies Program Newsletter* 57 (1998): 3–6, 9.

———. "Potlatch Arquitectónico." *Arquitectura Viva* July / Aug. 1997: 20–23.

———. "The Seduction of Bilbao." *Architecture* 86 (1997): 60–63.

Zunino, Maria Giulia. "Frank O. Gehry a Bilbao: Guggenheim Museum." *Abitare* March 1998: 126–45.

Newspapers

"Art Confronts Terrorism." *Jerusalem Post,* 19 Oct. 1997, Opinion, 6.

Aspden, Peter. "Spaced Out in Bilbao." *Financial Times,* 18 Oct. 1997, Arts, 8.

Baker, Kenneth. "The Great Wall of Chinese Art Staggering: Guggenheim Exhibition Is Ambitious—and Overwhelming." *San Francisco Chronicle,* 4 April 1998, final ed., Daily Datebook, 1(C).

Baldwin, Deborah. "Guggenheim's Spanish Port: Acquiring a Taste for Bilbao, the Museum's Gritty Riverside Home." *Washington Post,* 21 Dec. 1997, final ed., Travel, 1(E).

Ballard, J. G. "The 1990s in Review." *The Independent,* 28 Nov. 1999, Features, 2+.

Barrell, Sarah. "A Short Stay in Bilbao." *The Independent,* 7 June 1998, Features, 3.

———

"Basques March in Spain." *Washington Post*, 17 Oct. 1997, final ed., 32(A).

"Basques 'Sick' of ETA Violence: 300,000 Protest After Separatist Guerrillas Kill Police Officer." *Toronto Star*, 17 Oct. 1997, final ed., News, 20(A).

Bernthal, Ron. "Build It and They Will Come: New Guggenheim Museum an Unlikely Tourist Attraction in Basque City of Bilbao." *Toronto Sun*, 14 June 1998, final ed., Travel, T6.

Bey, Lee. "Gehry a 'Complete Original.' " *Chicago Sun-Times*, 4 Nov. 1999, late ed., NWS, 6.

Binney, Marcus. "Away with the Grime of Decay." *Times*, 12 April 1995, Features.

———. "Flagship of the Modern World." *Times*, 18 Oct. 1997, Features.

Black, Debra. "Building a Legacy." *Toronto Star*, 17 Oct. 1999, first ed., Life, 1+.

Bohlen, Celestine. "The Guggenheim's Scaled-Back Ambition." *New York Times*, 20 Nov. 2001. <http://nytimes.com>.

"Braced for Blockbuster." *South China Morning Post*, 18 May 1997, Agenda, 4.

Burns, Tom. "Basques Make a Dangerous Liaison." *Financial Times*, 18 Oct. 1997, Arts, 8.

———. "Tourism: Fresh Perceptions Taking Root." *Financial Times*, 9 July 1998, 4.

Bruce, Peter. "Museum Sets the Basques Ablaze." *Financial Times*, 15 Feb. 1992, Overseas news, 2(I).

Campbell, Robert. "Catching Up with Gehry's Masterpiece." *Boston Globe*, 22 Aug. 1999, Arts and Film, 6(N).

———. "Frank Gehry: From the Ground Up." *Boston Globe*, 27 Jan. 1999, Living, 1(C).

Castro, Alex Fernandez de. "Art Museum Polishes Bilbao's Image." *Daily Yomiuri*, 25 Nov. 1997, 10.

Cava, Marco R. della. "The 'Miracle' of Bilbao: Spanish City Pins Hopes on Dramatic New Art Museum." *USA TODAY*, 8 Oct. 1997, final ed., Life, 2(D).

Cork, Richard. "Big, Bold and Brilliant in Bilbao." *Times*, 21 Oct. 1997, Features.

Daly, Emma. "Where Blood Spilled, Art Rises." *Boston Globe*, 18 Oct. 1997, 2(A).

D' Arcy, Susan. "Basque in the Sun." *Sunday Times (London)*, 27 June 1999, Feature.

Dobrzynski, Judith H. "Hip Vs. Stately: The Tao of Two Museums. Interview with Philippe de Montebello and Thomas Krens." *New York Times*, 20 Feb. 2000, Arts and Leisure, sec. 2, 1+.

Dorment, Richard. "The Arts: Bilbao's Birth of a Wonder." *Daily Telegraph,*23 Oct. 1997, 24.

———. "Bilbao's Towering Tribute to the Arts: The Guggenheim Museum Will Become One of the Greatest Buildings of the 20th Century." *Daily Telegraph*, 17 Oct. 1997, International, 19.

———. "New Guggenheim Museum Perfect Showcase for Art." *Ottawa Citizen*, 18 Oct. 1997, final ed., News, 19(A).

"ETA Bombers Unbowed." *Herald (Glasgow)*, 18 Oct. 1997, 12.

"ETA Bombs Bilbao in Advance of Royal Visit." *Independent*, 18 Oct. 1997, News, 14.

Forgey, Benjamin. "A Gehry-Tale Image." *Washington Post* , 12 Sept. 1999, final ed., Arts, 1(G).

Foster, Hal. "Slouching Toward Bilbao." *Los Angeles Times*, 14 Oct., 2001, Book Review, 6–8.

Fox, Catherine. "Spain's Guggenheim Museum." *Atlanta Journal and Constitution*, 9 Nov. 1997, Arts, 1(K).

Gayford, Martin. "Where Next After Bilbao? Thomas Krens Tells Martin Gayford How He's Taking Museums Into the Next Century." *Daily Telegraph (London)*, 21 Nov. 1998, 2.

Giovannini, Joseph. "Art / Architecture." *New York Times*, 29 Aug. 1999, late ed., Arts and Leisure, sec. 2, 27.

Glaister, Dan. "Arts: Deal of the Decade." *Guardian*, 4 Oct. 1997, Features, 6.

Glancey, Jonathan. "Architecture: Basque in Glory." *Guardian*, 25 Oct. 1997, Weekend, 58.

Glauber, Bill. "Art as Business Boost: Guggenheim Museum in Bilbao, Spain, Opens to Public Tomorrow." *Gazette (Montreal)*, 18 Oct. 1997, final ed., 2(B).

Glueck, Grace. "Thinking Big at the Guggenheim." *New York Times*, 29 May 1988, late ed., Arts and Leisure, sec. 2,1+.

Gooch, Adela. "Fresh Twist to Guernica's Symbolic Torture." *Guardian*, 8 June 1996, Home, 3.

Goodman, Al. "Gehry Plans Another Architectural Surprise for Spain." *New York Times*, 15 July 1999, final ed., 2(E).

Griffith, Victoria. "Delighting in the Messiness of Life." *Financial Times*, 15 Jan. 2000, Perspectives, 3.

Guenaga, Aitor. "ETA mata a un policía vasco que impidió un atentado al Guggenheim." *El país*, 20 Oct. 1997, 14.

" 'Guernica' to Stay in Madrid." *New York Times*, 14 May 1997, final ed., sec. C, 12.

Hales, Linda. "Ahead of the Curve." *Washington Post*, 27 May 1999, final ed., Home, 12(T).

Hoge, Warren. "Bilbao's Cinderella Story." *New York Times*, 8 Aug. 1999, late ed., sec. 5, 14+.

Honan, William H. "Guggenheim's Orbit May Take in Spain." *New York Times*, 2 Oct. 1991, final ed., sec. C, 17.

Hopkins, Adam. "Bilbao Basques in Bright Beginnings." *Times*, 1 Aug. 1998, Features.

"Icons on Wheels." *Irish Times*, 23 Nov. 1999, Arts, 14.

Islam, Faisal. "Breathing New Life Into Our Ailing Inner Cities." *Observer*, 11 July 1999, Business, 8.

Kaufman, Jason Edward. "Bilbao's Guggenheim: New Colossus." *Washington Post*, 26 Oct. 1997, final ed., Arts, 2(G).

Kimmelman, Michael. "Critic's Notebook: The Museum as Work of Art." *New York Times*, 20 Oct. 1997, final ed., 1(E).

———. "Critic's Notebook: To Serve Art, Not Overwhelm It." *New York Times*, 5 Feb. 1998, final ed., 1(E).

———. "What on Earth Is the Guggenheim Up To?" *New York Times*, 14 Oct. 1990, late ed., Arts and Leisure, sec. 2, 1+.

Lawson-Johnston, Peter. Letter. *Wall Street Journal*, 19 May 1994, 15(A).

Lewis, Anthony. "At Home Abroad: Engine for Change." *New York Times*, 17 April 1999, final ed., 17(A).

Lewis, Roger K. "Gehry's Provocative Architecture Proving Irresistable to the Media." *Washington Post*, 1 Nov. 1997, final ed., 1(F).

Lieberman, Paul. "After the Success of the Guggenheim in Bilbao, Spain, Small Cities Are Banking on Art Museums to Rev Up Economies." *Los Angeles Times*, 20 June 1999, home ed., Calendar, 4.

Litt, Steven. "Museum Has Strong Start Despite Some Controversy." *Plain Dealer*, 19 Oct. 1997, Arts and Living, 31.

———. "A Spell Is Cast: Basques, U. S. Architect Collaborate on a Masterpiece." *Plain Dealer*, 19 Oct. 1997, Arts and Living, 11.

Mack, Linda. "New Gehry Museum's Skin Moves With Wind." *Star Tribune (Minneapolis, MN)*, 26 Oct 1997, Entertainment, 4(F).

MacMillan, Kyle. "Two Dazzling Buildings Redefine Art Museum." *Omaha World-Herald*, 21 March 1999, sunrise ed., Entertainment, 22.

MacRitchie, Lynn. "Basque Sculptor Carves Out a Niche in Bilbao: Eduardo Chillida's Retrospective Has an Effortless Monumentality." *Financial Times*, 19 May 1999, Arts, 18.

McEwen, John. "The Arts: Spain Sketches the Future Art." *Sunday Telegraph*, 7 Dec. 1997, 12.

McCrum, Robert. "Where to Go to See a Masterpiece: The Bilbao Guggenheim." *Observer*, 12 Oct. 1997, Life, 14.

Melvin, Jeremy. "The Shape of Democracy." *Guardian*, 14 Sept. 1998, Features, 10.

Monahan, Jane. "Showcase for the Moderns in Bilbao." *Times*, 13 Nov. 1992, Features.

Moore, Rowan. "The Arts: Basques Bask in a Glow of Millenial Fever." *Daily Telegraph*, 5 April 1995, 18.

———. "The Arts: Heroic, Chaotic, Fabulous." *Sunday Telegraph*, 13 April 1997, 7.

Moore, Rowan. "The Arts: Poised Between Flowering and Collapse with His Disney Hall Plans in Limbo." *Daily Telegraph*, 21 June 1997, 7.

Moore, Susan. "Guggenheim Megalomania." *Financial Times*, 23 May 1992, Arts, 17.

———

Moore, Susan. "The Real Cost of a Higher Profile." *Financial Times*, 3 June 1995, Collecting, 16.

Morrison, Richard. "Put Some Fire in the Belly of an Architect." *Times*, 15 Jan. 1999, Features.

Muschamp, Herbert. "Blueprint: The Shock of the Familiar." *New York Times*, 13 Dec. 1998, final ed., sec. 6, 61.

———. "Critic's Choices: Heroic Spaces and the Perfect Spoon." *New York Times*, 7 Sept. 1997, final ed., sec. 2, 84.

———. "Culture's Power Houses: The Museum Becomes an Engine of Urban Redesign." *New York Times*, 21 April 1999, late ed., 1(G).

———. "The Guggenheim's East Side Vision." *New York Times*, 17 April 2000, late ed.: 23(A).

———. "The Miracle in Bilbao." *New York Times*, 7 Sept. 1997, late ed., sec. 6, 54+.

Nash, Elizabeth. "Art Is the Politics of the Possible." *Independent*, 26 April 1997, Arts and Books, 5.

———. "Basques Denied 'Guernica.' " *Independent*, 14 May 1997, International, 8.

———. "For Whom the Bell Is Still Tolling: The Guggenheim Museum in Bilbao Has Focused the Attention of the World on the Basque Country." *Independent*, 16 Nov. 1997, Features, 14.

———. "Never Mind the Art, Enjoy the Architecture." *Independent*, 13 July 1997, International, 15.

"News in Brief: Guernica Stays Put." *Guardian*, 14 May 1997, Foreign, 11.

"Nervion centre." *Guardian*, 23 Oct. 1999, Travel, 8.

"The Newest Guggenheim: Futuristic Art Museum Helps Put Fresh Face on Spain's Basque Region." *Houston Chronicle*, 17 Oct. 1997, 1.

Ourousoff, Nicolai. "I'm Frank Gehry and This Is How I See the World: For the Architect Who Made Bilbao a Household Word, It's All About Freedom and Contol." *Los Angeles Times*, 25 Oct. 1998, home ed., Magazine, 17.

Ourousoff, Nicolai. "It Doesn't Get Much Better Than This: The Opening of the Getty Center in L.A. and the Guggenheim Museum in Bilbao, Spain, Made 1997 a Memorable

Year, Perhaps Even a Historic One." *Los Angeles Times*, 21 Dec. 1997, home ed., Calendar, 63.
———. "The Architect's New Museum in Bilbao, Spain, Emerges as a Testament to One Man's Optimism Amid a Landscape of Industrial Decay." *Los Angeles Times*, 2 June 1997, Calendar, F1.
Pearman, Hugh. "A Vision of the 20th Century." *Sunday Times*, 19 Oct. 1997, Features.
Pizzichini, Lilian. "What Frank Gehry Did Next." *Independent*, 14 Dec. 1997, Features.
"Policeman Dies Foiling Bomb Attack on Royal Opening of Bilbao Museum." *Guardian*, 16 Oct. 1997, Foreign, 14.
Rawsthorn, Alice. "Buildings to Celebrate." *Financial Times*, 23 Dec. 1999, first ed., The Arts, 14.
Reid, T. R. "The Art of Rejuvenation: Museum Puts Bilbao Back On Spain's Economic and Cultural Maps." *Washington Post*, 31 March 1999, 16+(A).
Riding, Alan. "The Basques Get Modern: A Gleaming New Guggenheim for Grimy Bilbao." *New York Times*, 24 June 1997, final ed., sec. C, 9.
———. "Gehry's Guggenheim Raises a Depressed City's Spirits." *San Diego Union-Tribune*, 20 July 1997, 9(H).
———. "Guggenheim Built in Spain Opens Under Militant Cloud." *New York Times*, 19 Oct. 1997, final ed., sec. 1, 8.
———. "Guggenheim Represents City's Hope for New Image." *Times-Picayune*, 19 Oct. 1997, 31(A).
Rinaldi, Ray Mark. "Guggenheim Museum Is a Bit of New York on the Nervion." *St. Louis-Dispatch*, 19 April 1998, Travel and Leisure, 8(T).
———. "Spain's Basque Region Hides a Great Museum." *Houston Chronicle*, 3 May 1998, Travel, 12.
Smith, Roberta. "A Spaniard Who Has Carved a Niche Beyond Modern and Minimal." *New York Times*, 4 July 1997, final ed., sec. C, 24.
Temin, Christine. "The Guggenheim Bilbao Has Created a Sublime Expression of American Culture—And a New Destination for the Art World." *Boston Globe*, 8 March 1998, Arts and Films, 1(N).

———

"Tension Marks Guggenheim Opening: Opening Day Jitters." *ABC News* 18 Oct. 1997. <http://www.abcnews.com>.

"Thousands Protest at ETA Killing." *Herald (Glasgow)*, 17 Oct. 1997, 12.

Tremlett, Giles. "Portrait of a City's New Emblem." *Times*, 19 March 1998, Features.

Tuck, Andrew. "Basquing in the Glory." *Independent*, 24 Aug. 1997, Features, 14.

"Two Million." *Financial Times*, 5 July 1999, Shorts, 1.

Updike, Robin. "Spain's Guggenheim Museum Has Connections with Seattle." *Seattle Times*, 7 July 1997, final ed., Arts and Entertainment, 1(E).

Varadarajan, Tunku. "Art Museum Shopping Draws Critics." *Times*, 1 March 1997, Overseas news.

Vogel, Carol. "Guggenheim Announces Record Gift, $50 Million." *New York Times* 15 April 1998, final ed., sec. E, 1.

———. "New Attractions: Bilbao and Art." *New York Times* 19 Dec. 1997, final ed., sec. E, 38.

———. "Revlon's Chairman Donates $10 Million to the Guggenheim." *New York Times* 20 Jan. 1994, final ed., sec. C, 15.

Wallach, Amei. "A Museum Makeover: New Guggenheim." *Los Angeles Times*, 16 June 1992, Calendar, 1(F).

Webster, Justin. "The Basque Country: Art Museum Played Key Role in Plans." *Independent*, 14 Dec. 1993, 16.

———. "Letter from Barcelona: 'My Fault Is that I Am an Independent Artist, Not a Carpet': Why the Success of the Bilbao Guggenheim Worries People in Barcelona." *Independent*, 16 Aug. 1998, Features, 3.

White, David. "A New Face to the World." *Financial Times*, 27 May 1997, Survey, 4.

———. "Police Foil Grenade Attack on Spanish King." *Financial Times*, 16 Oct. 1997, News, 3.

Wickers, David. "Shining Star." *Sunday Times*, 19 Oct. 1997, Features.

Woodworth, Paddy. "The Wow of Bilbao." *Irish Times*, 30 March 2002, Magazine, 20–22.

Worsley, Giles. "Turning Points: Fifty Works that Shaped the Century." *Daily Telegraph (London)*, 13 Feb. 1999, 6.
"Wow! Bilbao!" *Irish Times*, 25 Oct. 1997, Weekend, 60.

Websites

<http://www.bilbao.net>
<http://www.guggenheim.org>

Index

A

B

C

D

G

H

I

J

M

N

O

P

Q

R

S

T

U

V

W

Y

W

Colophon

This book was edited by Dave Blake and indexed by Lawrence Feldman. It was laid out and produced by Gunnlaugur SE Briem, who also designed the typeface, BriemAnvil.

The Basque Studies textbook series

1. Basque Cinema: An Introduction
2. Basque Culture: Anthropological Perspectives
3. Basque Cyberculture: From Digital Euskadi to CyberEuskalherria
4. Basque Diaspora; Migration and Transnational Identity
5. Basque Economy: From Industrialization to Globalization
6. Basque Gender Studies
7. Basque Sociolinguistics; Language, Society, and Culture
8. Basque Sociology; Society, Identity, and Politics
9. Guggenheim Bilbao Museoa: Museums, Architecture, and City Renewal
10. Modern Basque History: Eighteenth Century to the Present
11. Waking the Hedgehog; The Literary Universe of Bernardo Atxaga

www.ingramcontent.com/pod-product-compliance
Lightning Source LLC
LaVergne TN
LVHW050624100826
845148LV00011B/1725

* 9 7 8 1 8 7 7 8 0 2 0 6 5 *